CRACKING DaVINCI'S CODE

JAMES L. GARLOW
PETER JONES

Victor®

The Bible Teacher's Teacher

COOK COMMUNICATIONS MINISTRIES
Colorado Springs, Colorado • Paris, Ontario
KINGSWAY COMMUNICATIONS LTD
Eastbourne, England

Victor® is an imprint of
Cook Communications Ministries, Colorado Springs, CO 80918
Cook Communications, Paris, Ontario
Kingsway Communications, Eastbourne, England

CRACKING DA VINCI'S CODE (Abridged)
© 2005 by James L. Garlow and Peter Jones

First Printing, 2005 - Second Printing, 2005
Printed in Canada

2 3 4 5 6 7 8 9 10 Printing/Year 09 08 07 06 05

Cover design: by Koechel Peterson & Associates, Inc., Minneapolis, Minnesota
Cover art: *The Last Supper* by Leonardo da Vinci is Public Domain.
Photograph: Public Domain © SuperStock

The Da Vinci Code is published by Doubleday, a division of Random House, Inc., 1745
Broadway, New York, New York. Copyright © 2003 by Dan Brown. All rights reserved.

ISBN: 0781443563

CONTENTS

CHAPTER 1
THE CODE THAT SHOOK THE WORLD

*"What I mean," Teabing countered, "is that almost
everything our fathers taught us about Christ is false.
As are the stories about the Holy Grail."*
Dan Brown, The Da Vinci Code†

Everything you've ever learned about Jesus Christ is false.
Is this possible?

Leigh Teabing is an expert in the ancient trail leading to
the Holy Grail. A former British royal historian, Teabing
moved to France to personally search through churches for
clues leading to the Grail. He is a multimillionaire descen-
dent of the first duke of Lancaster and lives in a
seventeenth-century castle with two private lakes.

One more thing about Leigh Teabing: He does not exist.

Teabing is one of the fanciful characters in Dan Brown's
runaway best seller, *The Da Vinci Code*. A fun, fast-paced sus-
pense novel, *The Da Vinci Code* debuted at number one on the
New York Times best-seller list, quickly hit the number-one
position with every major best-seller list in the United States,
and has been translated into more than forty languages. A
year after its publication, *The Da Vinci Code* had sold more
than six million hardback copies. Clearly, the fictional Leigh
Teabing—as well as Brown's main character, Robert
Langdon—has a strong platform from which to share his con-
victions about Jesus Christ.

---

† All subsequent references to this book will be designated by page number only, for
example (235).

But Dan Brown is very real. And the ideas he presents about Christianity, spoken through Langdon, Teabing, and other characters in his book, are causing many to question what they have always believed to be true about Jesus.

It is time to separate fact from fiction.

The Da Vinci Code starts out with a ghastly murder in the Louvre Museum in Paris. The police call in Robert Langdon, a professor of religious symbology at Harvard, to help unravel the mysterious clues left near the corpse. On and around the body are riddles, which—when solved by Langdon and police cryptographer Sophie Neveu—lead to clues hidden in plain sight in the art of Leonardo da Vinci.

Langdon learns that the murdered curator of the Louvre, Jacques Saunière, was not only the estranged grandfather of Neveu, he was also the Grand Master of an ancient society entrusted with guarding a secret that, if revealed, would threaten the very existence of the Christian church. Saunière died protecting the location of the proof of the Holy Grail.

Racing through the streets of Paris, to Teabing's exotic estate, to London aboard an unregistered flight, Langdon and Neveu try to stay one step ahead of the French police, an albino killer, and a mysterious man who is orchestrating this deadly search for the Grail. Intricate symbols and riddles lead Langdon and Neveu to the exciting conclusion, where the location of the Grail is revealed.

THE BIG COVER-UP

Throughout the novel, Robert Langdon teaches Sophie Neveu about the code—how to find the "true" Holy Grail. We find out that the Grail is not what we thought it was. The Grail, according to Langdon, is such a great secret that, if it were exposed, Christianity as we know it today would cease to exist. But it is not an *object* that author Dan Brown, through his protagonist Langdon, wants to reveal to us. And it is not just the secret location of this religious icon that so many have died to protect. The very substance of the Grail itself is at the core of this mystery. In the past, we have been led to believe that the Holy Grail—if it ever existed—is the cup Christ drank from at his last supper, and then was used by Joseph of Arimathea to collect blood from the crucified Christ. But according to Dan Brown's characters— Langdon and Teabing—the true Grail is not a thing, it is a person.

The Holy Grail is Mary Magdalene ... the mother of the royal bloodline of Jesus Christ (253).[1]

Brown asserts that Mary Magdalene and Jesus were sexual partners and had a child together. When Jesus died, Mary fled from the other disciples, who were jealous of her relationship with Jesus, and lived in a Jewish community in France with their child. There is documented proof of this assertion, according to Brown, proof that has been guarded since the days of the Crusades by a secret organization known as the Priory of Sion. Hints of this secret can be found hidden in paintings and drawings by da Vinci and other artists throughout history, if only one knows how and where to look.

These theories are not new. As a matter of fact, Brown freely references other books in *The Da Vinci Code*, books that explore this theory of Mary Magdalene and Jesus. Most prominent among these other works is *Holy Blood, Holy Grail*, a 1982 release by Michael Baigent, Richard Leigh, and Henry Lincoln. (Brown's fictional character Leigh Teabing's name is an anagram of Baigent and Leigh.) The hypothesis that Jesus produced a child, or children, with Mary has been around for centuries. So why do we feel it necessary now to respond to it? Why did we set out to crack da Vinci's "code"?

JESUS: LOVER AND FATHER?

Many of the millions who have read *The Da Vinci Code* have enjoyed it solely as an entertaining mystery story. The action is tight—cliff-hangers at the end of just about every chapter propel the reader forward. Watching Langdon and Neveu solve each new riddle makes for a book that is hard to put down. And Brown uses a standard formula in romance writing: over-the-top characters against an exotic, but flat, background to create a story that appeals to both men and women, evidenced by the number of both sexes who have bought and read the book so far. Many of these readers have already moved on to the next book in their "to-be-read" pile.

Yet there are many readers of Brown's book who are now confused about just who Jesus really is. These readers are turning away from what they thought to be true to grasp a mangled mass of bizarre claims cleverly portrayed as a work of history in a work of fiction.

Cracking Da Vinci's Code is for you if you have stopped to ponder Brown's "code" woven into his novel. It is for you if you are now questioning all you have learned about Jesus. We are writing for you if you are now saying, "I once thought of Jesus as the Son of God, but I guess I was wrong. He is simply a man after all." For your sake, and his, we feel we must respond.

David Klinghoffer, writing in the *National Review*, sees the great danger in Brown's story:

> What's at stake in *The Da Vinci Code* is nothing less than traditional Christianity itself.… The founder of Christianity had a daughter, Sarah, by Mary Magdalene. If true, this theory would overturn some of the central beliefs of Christians.[2]

If true. Two very important words to consider. If Dan Brown is simply making up a plotline and including far-fetched fantasy, then this response would not be necessary. But Brown maintains that all he is writing is real. While being interviewed on NBC's *Today Show,* Brown defended the material he used in the book:

> MATT LAUER: How much of this is based on reality in terms of things that actually occurred?
> DAN BROWN: Absolutely all of it. Obviously, Robert Langdon is fictional, but all of the art, architecture, secret rituals, secret societies—all of that is historical fact.[3]

There is a reason Brown wants to stress that his work is factual. He wants you to come away with a new mind-set.

"One of the aspects that I try very hard to incorporate in my books is that of learning," said Brown in an interview with *Bookpage* magazine. "When you finish the book, like it or not, you've learned a ton."[4] So Brown the novelist is also a teacher. And, like many good teachers, he begins his lesson by calling into question what you always thought was unquestionable.

- Jesus had sexual relations with Mary Magdalene?
- Our Bible is the construct of Constantine's political whims?
- The church has it in for women?
- Jesus was "voted" divine at the Council of Nicæa?

We can't honestly embrace these ideas, can we? After all, we have historical facts to show each of these claims to be false. Brown, however, has his own ideas about history and how much it can be trusted.

"It's interesting to note," says Brown, "that since

the beginning of recorded time, history has been written by the 'winners' (those societies and belief systems that conquered and survived).

"Many historians now believe (as do I) that in gauging the historical accuracy of a given concept, we should first ask ourselves a far deeper question: How historically accurate is history itself?"[5]

HISTORY OR HOAX?

With that single question, Brown tosses out all traditional historical fact, everything we have built on through the centuries. *How accurate is history?* This is a pivotal recurring question in our postmodern society. It is also an echo of Pilate's question when faced with an innocent man he was condemning to death: "What is truth?" (John 18:38). By tossing aside the notion that there is such a thing as objective truth, we have nothing solid to hold on to. Thus we find ourselves adrift in a sea of confusion and doubt. To the contemporary audience, any method of recording or rewriting history is just fine. Brown discounts much of accepted history because it was written by the church. And winners write history. Yet, he says everything he presents in *The Da Vinci Code* is "historical fact." So who are the new "winners" that Brown relies on for his historical facts?

These winners are obviously those who agree with his version of Jesus, Mary Magdalene, and the teachings of the Bible. He couches these beliefs in symbols, hidden messages in paintings, and ancient documents that were not even accepted as authentic at the time of their writing. Many of these so-called "facts" on which Brown hangs his theories are easily discounted as false.

Our main purpose in these pages is twofold. First, we want to reveal the real "code" that Brown has weaved throughout his story. What is this code? How can you recognize it in today's world? What does this code have to do with you and your beliefs? We will show you that Brown's code is far more dangerous to your soul than the fictional da Vinci code.

Second, we want to respond to the Holy Grail story. Perhaps it will surprise you to learn that we, Jim Garlow and Peter Jones, believe in the "Holy Grail." And it may further shock you to hear us say that Dan Brown almost has it right. We are going to reveal to you not only *what* the Grail is, but *where it is today*.

CHAPTER 2
SECRET KNOWLEDGE VERSUS GOD'S GREAT IDEA

Our ancient heritage and our very physiologies tell us sex is natural—a cherished route to spiritual fulfillment— and yet modern religion decries it as shameful, teaching us to fear our sexual desire as the hand of the devil (310).

The Da Vinci Code is not a sex book. And yet it is a book very much about sex.

As we progress through the novel, we find a church that is so power-hungry it suppresses a natural, pleasurable act given by God to be fully enjoyed by humans.

- Is it true that the sexual union between man and woman is the only way to "achieve *gnosis*—knowledge of the divine" (308)?
- Is it true that the church has repositioned sex as evil in order to combat a threat to its power (309)?
- Is sex "a mystical, spiritual act … [whereby one can] find that spark of divinity that man can only achieve through union with the sacred feminine" (310)?
- Is it true that the "Hieros Gamos [sacred marriage] ritual is not a perversion … [but] a deeply sacrosanct ceremony" used by the early church (309)?

Reading *The Da Vinci Code* reminded me (Peter) of the week I spent at the Parliament of the World's Religions in Chicago in 1993. Eight thousand delegates were there, representing 125 different religions. We sang "Leaning on the Everlasting Arms," but the song failed to identify whose arms they were. I popped my head into the darkened "meditation room" and listened briefly to the unfamiliar chanting sounds.

I made a quick break for the exit when the leaders of the Fellowship of Isis "seminar" announced that they were about to enter "the second chamber." The first chamber was enough for me. In it the audience wailed, as if possessed, in ecstatic praise of the Goddess. The only spirituality I didn't see all week was that of biblical Christianity.

THE "SACROSANCT CEREMONY"

One of the most powerful scenes in *The Da Vinci Code* takes place in early spring in windswept Normandy. Sophie Neveu discovers her grandfather, Jacques Saunière, engaged in a secret sex ritual in the basement of his old country house, as masked worshippers look on, rocking back and forth and chanting. The men are dressed in black, the women in white. Later Robert Langdon explains to a distraught Sophie that the ritual she saw was Hieros Gamos, "sacred marriage," and that it was "not about sex, it was about spirituality ... not a perversion ... [but] a deeply sacrosanct ceremony" (308–309).

In this scene is found the only extended description of a religious experience in the entire novel. Here Brown illustrates "the sacred feminine."

The word *sacred* means "special" or "holy"; *feminine*, in this context, stands for "goddess spirituality." *The Da Vinci Code* explains why the rite of holy marriage fell on hard times: "Holy men who had once required sexual union with their female counterparts to commune with God now feared their natural sexual urges as the work of the devil" (125), and thus the rite was banished by the narrow-minded church.

The Da Vinci Code does accurately describe a spirituality

that took place in history and claimed to be true Christianity. The non-Christian pagan mysteries also had such rites of initiation. Such a ritual takes place in the basement of the home of Jacques Saunière, who "was no Christian" (140). In spite of this fact, Saunière is one of the models of spirituality in the novel.

The goal of the ritual is to gain, at the moment of orgasm in a sexual union with a woman, spiritual completeness and gnosis, or secret knowledge (308). *The Da Vinci Code* does not say how the woman gains knowledge, since she is only a "chalice" in this rite (309), but the male, with the help of the chanting crowd, "could achieve a climactic instant when his mind went totally blank and he could see God" (309).

Is *The Da Vinci Code* just an interesting "historical" novel, or is its research on these ancient practices serving a contemporary purpose? To us, the answer is obvious. The novel is making a case for an old form of spirituality that is reappearing in the twenty-first century.

Someone has said, "We are not dealing with fringe religious groups … but with a broad-based effort to influence and restructure our whole society … 'a new society forming within the heart of the old.'"[1] The earth is shuddering beneath our feet. As a Roman Catholic writer states, "We are witnessing a spiritual revolution of great magnitude in the whole world … the rise of a new school of mysticism [even] within Christianity."[2]

But why is this happening? Setting aside the cynical question of motives … because people do yearn for spiritual transformation!

The Post-Christian Mantra

For Jacques Saunière, transformation comes through spiritual delirium. The mind goes blank, and other sensations take over. Today we call this "altered states of consciousness." Orgasm and chanting constitute one avenue to ecstatic, mindless experience. There are many others.

Many people today equate this experience with being or feeling "spiritual." An academic discipline called "transpersonal psychology" studies and promotes these "technologies of the sacred" as the wave of our spiritual future and the only hope for the planet.[3] Apparently, what drove second-century "Christian" Gnostics is driving more and more of us. Our post-Christian culture is rediscovering this ancient spirituality. As one writer on Jesus said, "Jesus won't become a national figure [in America] unless he can move outside Christianity."[4]

The first goal of spiritual ecstasy is mindlessness, a state sought in Hindu and Buddhist meditation, often through the repetition of a "mantra." The term *mantra* comes from two Sanskrit words, *man* ("to think") and *tra* ("to be liberated from"). Loose translation: "You are at your best when you are not thinking."

Hinduism, the so-called path to mystical experience, involves getting beyond the intellect or "killing the mind."[5] A contemporary New Age teacher says, "The enemy of meditation is the mind."[6] The ancient Gnostics taught the same. One of the Gnostic scrolls calls for "an entry into that which is silent, the place which has no need for utterance nor for comprehending."[7] The Jesus of another Gnostic scroll commands his disciples, "Be filled with the Spirit, but be lacking in reason or intellect (logos)."[8]

Why the escape from the mind? The simple answer: to get life-changing knowledge (gnosis).

WHY IS MONA LISA SMILING?

The astute reader of *The Da Vinci Code* will notice the mention of the word *androgynous*. At the sex ritual, the cult members are wearing "androgynous masks" (308); Yahweh is presented as an ancient name containing the idea of an "androgynous physical union";[9] Leonardo da Vinci's Mona Lisa is "smiling" (101). "Why? Because Mona Lisa really stands for Amon and L'Isa (Isis), the androgynous pair, so that the painting presents an image that is "neither male nor female ... [but] carries a subtle message of androgyny ... a fusing of both" (121). The Mona Lisa smiles because she has gnosis.

The Joining of the Opposites

The liberation of sex is not the only effect of such spirituality. Long before the appearance of *The Da Vinci Code*, Gnostic believers were "reconstructed in androgynous unity" in the bridal chamber.[10] In other words, something happened to them that changed the way they thought about themselves. Such transformation is the goal of all these techniques. Shirley MacLaine said the very point of life was to know ourselves as we truly are—"androgynous, a perfect balance."[11] What do Shirley MacLaine and Dan Brown know that most of us do not know?

Knowing oneself to be both male and female changes everything, according to this esoteric tradition. Reconstructing God-given sexuality appears in this spirituality to be at the top of the agenda. In undergoing this transformation, one "joins the opposites," the classic phrase for gnosis. This means that in the irrational state of altered consciousness, all the normal distinctions of everyday life—not merely the sexual distinctions—fall away: "The blade and chalice. Fused as one" (446). This concept is further expressed in Jacques Saunière's "passion for dualism ... Everything in pairs ... Male female. Black nested within white" (323).

This is the deep Gnostic experience of liberation. The joining of the opposites means that those so joined rise above all distinctions, which are mere illusion, or, as the Hindus say, maya.

This, they would insist, must especially be true of what Christians traditionally distinguish as "good" and "evil."

No-Guilt "Liberation"

There is more to a Gnostic spiritual high than trancelike ecstasy or physical orgasm. There is an experience of dominion, a great sense of empowerment, fraught with great danger. Going beyond the limitations of your mind also takes you beyond rational definitions of right and wrong. You are no longer subject to external laws of good and evil. Instead, you become the judge. Everything about you seems okay, and all your instincts must be valid.

The ultimate goal of this mystical experience of oneness with all things is clear—to deny guilt. In this system, there is no place for sin. According to Robert Langdon, "It was man, not God, who created the concept of … sin" (238).

By embracing evil, mystical spirituality produces a temporary, counterfeit euphoria of virtual redemption and relief from guilt. But in truth, it merely deadens the God-given mechanism of moral pain that would otherwise alert us to our worst selves.

Perhaps Brown has not thought through all the implications of his message, but *The Da Vinci Code* is a deliberate and powerful propaganda tool for this view of spirituality.

However, in claiming that the early church used "sex to commune directly with God" (309), the novel goes too far. There is not one hint of either condoning or acknowledging—let alone encouraging—such practice in the books of the New Testament.

The gospel of Philip does not represent the spirituality of Jesus and the earliest Christianity. The external evidence alone insists that it had to be an extremist Gnostic perversion of both biblical spirituality and sexuality. As we'll see in future chapters, Gnostic "Christians" were not the original thing—they sought to transform Christianity into one of the pagan mystery religions so popular in the ancient world.

CHRISTIAN SEXUALITY AND SPIRITUALITY

Biblical spirituality is very different from Gnostic spirituality. There are no secret chambers, no drumming, dancing, drugs, or technologies to produce altered states of consciousness. In fact, Jesus commanded that there be no babbling of mantras (Matthew 6:7). There are no secret rituals or ceremonies. On the contrary, unbelievers are openly invited to participate in the church's celebrations (1 Corinthians 14:22–25; an exception is made for the Lord's Supper, which is for believers only).

The tone of openness was set by Jesus, who stated, "I have spoken openly to the world. I have always taught in synagogues and in the temple, where all Jews come together. I have said nothing in secret" (John 18:20 ESV). He commanded His disciples to preach from the rooftops (Matthew 10:27).

Sex: What Was God Thinking?

Some have tried to insist that sex was created only for procreation. But did God have something more planned for us when he created us with sexual desires? The answer is a resounding yes! Sexual union and pleasure is a God-endowed part of our physical, emotional, and spiritual blueprints.

But, like so many things God created for our enjoyment, we have corrupted and warped his plans. Instead of abundant pleasure and joy, our ways result in pain, disappointment, and—ultimately—separation from God.

Agape versus Eros

I (Jim) wrote my master's thesis on the Greek word *agape*, contrasting it with *eros*. No honest woman wants to be loved only erotically, as in eros—only for her looks. Eros loves only for what it can get out of the other person. When there is no more to get, the eros love is gone.

C. S. Lewis writes in *The Four Loves* about this type of selfish, sexually driven emotion:

> We use a most unfortunate idiom when we say, of a lustful man prowling the streets, that he "wants a woman." Strictly speaking, a woman is just what he does not want. He wants a pleasure for which a woman happens to be the necessary piece of apparatus. How much he cares about the woman as such may be gauged by his attitude to her five minutes after the fruition (one does not keep the carton after one has smoked the cigarettes).[12]

This essentially is the form of love Brown holds up as the highest form in *The Da Vinci Code*—that of classic paganism. With no connection between the Creator and the created, there is no reason to value individuals. Follow Dan Brown's thesis, and women will at best mutually participate in fulfilling eros-driven lust. At least antispiritual, if not antifeminine, such a worldview reduces sexuality to the merely physical.

Deep within every person there is a longing to be loved with agape love: that is, loved because we have intrinsic value; loved because we are created by God. God loves us with this agape love, and we are to love each other the same way. The Bible, the church, and Christian tradition, with their insistence on loving others with agape love, value people, who are treated with dignity and respect.

Is the Bible Antisex?

It would seem, at least from Brown's point of view, that the Bible and the church are both antisex. When Langdon informs the impressionable Sophie that the church is against sex, is he historically correct? Before looking at the church's view, let's see what the Bible has to say on the subject of sex.

We have two books: One is an engaging novel by Dan Brown; the other is the Bible. Both talk about sex. It is not the central message of either—yet it plays a significant role in both. The Bible has numerous key concepts regarding sex and sexual expression. And this Bible, being the source of all truth for the church, is full of beautiful references to sexual pleasure between man and woman. As a matter of fact, the Bible is an advocate of maximum sexual pleasure.

In Genesis 26:8 (NLT), Isaac is seen "fondling" his wife. Proverbs 5:18–19 encourages some rather explicit sexual enjoyment between husband and wife. And the Song of Songs (Song of Solomon) in the Old Testament is nothing less than an erotic love poem filled with all sorts of sexual expression.

In the New Testament, the references to sexual activity are not as poetically written. Nevertheless, in 1 Corinthians 7:1–6, Paul tells husbands and wives that they no longer own their bodies; rather, the husband's body belongs also to his wife, and the wife's also to her husband. In other words, they are to seek mutual satisfaction in their lovemaking. Furthermore, the marriage bed is treasured and honored as pure (see Hebrews 13:4). Sexual activities and pleasure are normal, expected, and encouraged within a marriage.

The Bible gives the church and individual believers principles for every aspect of life. Yet Brown ignores the positive teachings the Bible offers on sexual expression, substituting instead a ritual sex orgy (the Hieros Gamos) as the highest form of physical and spiritual pleasure. In doing so, he cheapens the luxurious experience God intended for us.

Is the Church Antisex?

According to *The Da Vinci Code*, the church is the grand oppressor of sex. Brown says that "the natural sexual union between man and woman through which each became spiritually whole … had been recast as a shameful act" (125). Their motive, he further explains, was to "'reeducate' the pagan and feminine-worshipping religions" (125).

Is Brown correct in his assessment of the church's view of sex? Does he accurately portray the historical Christian view of sex? The answer to the question is resoundingly more complex than *The Da Vinci Code* would have us believe.

While the Bible extols the joys and delights of marital sexual expression, some of the early church leaders immediately after the biblical period (AD 100) wrote in response to the cultural influences and conflicting understanding of their day. In his prolific writings, Augustine vacillated (in part because he was so filled with regret about his own pre-Christian immorality) between a condemning tone regarding sexual expression and strong affirmations of the role of marriage.

Some of the early church fathers wrote glowingly about the value of marriage, stating that within marriage, the couple partnered with God in creation. Julian of Eclanum, who carried on a vigorous debate with Augustine on the topic, expressed a distinctively biblical theme—that sexual expression between a husband and wife was intrinsically good since it was created by God.

Was Sex the "Original Sin"?

One example of Brown's inaccurate representation is Langdon's statement equating the sex act with "original sin." Once again, he selects the aberration and makes it the norm. A handful of the early church fathers did mistakenly believe that original sin was the sex act itself, but by far most did not, despite what *The Da Vinci Code* would have us believe (125).

Even though certain church fathers seem to have had a view of sex that did not match the Bible's teaching of maximum sexual fulfillment, their motivation could just as well have been sincerely (though misguided) for the spiritual well-being of their flocks. Arbitrarily and summarily assigning them the motive of politics and trying to control others is logically flawed and a stereotyped generalization.

SEX AS THE "DIVINE MOMENT"

Surprisingly, *The Da Vinci Code* is accurate in one of its portrayals of sexual expression. Brown is correct in describing the "divine-ness" or "divinity" of the sex act. He contends that it is in sexual union that God is experienced (308). But he is not correct for the reasons he believes.

First, we have to understand that the God of the Bible, though called our heavenly Father, has no gender—he has no genitalia, no X or Y chromosomes. God is spirit (see John 4:24), and the mystery of his person goes way beyond anything we humans can imagine. It is in that sense—in terms of his spiritual nature—that the Bible describes us as created "in his image" (Genesis 1:27). He is the person from whom our "personness" is derived, both male and female.

That's not to say we should describe him as androgynous. God created male and female genders; they don't define him. He created us "male and female" for a number of reasons, one of which was to express in the created universe some diverse elements that reflect his own character. So even while the Bible most often refers to God by masculine names and pronouns (such as "Father" and "he"), sometimes he is compared to a mother holding a newborn or to a hen guarding her chicks (see Matthew 23:37; Isaiah 49:15).

When a man and a woman come together sexually in "one flesh" (Genesis 2:24), they become a more complete expression of the infinite spectrum of God's characteristics. This is a crucial aspect of the amazing power—the indescribable magnetism—of sex. It is meant to be a response to God's potent stamp on the core of our beings.

It is this spiritual dimension of the pleasure and pull of

sexual expression that sanctifies sex. The result of the male-female union is not some androgynous entity. Men remain spectacularly male and masculine. Women remain wonderfully female and feminine. Unlike paganism's fascination with androgyny, the Bible affirms fully the magnificent differences of maleness and femaleness.

God's Design for Sex

Our sexuality and our spirit are inexplicably and profoundly intertwined. We are—at our core—spirit beings, created in God's image. So our sexuality is likewise at that same core—it must be, because we are more than animals in our nature. That is why sexuality cannot be perceived as some mere tangent for us humans, as if it were something removed from our spirit.

In order for the act of sexual expression between a man and woman to be fully representative of the spectrum of the characteristics of God, a male and female must be one in totality—and that includes oneness not merely physically, but oneness emotionally, spiritually, and psychologically. That oneness is not something experienced for a moment—it is lifelong. There is a phrase for this unique unity of being—it is called the covenant of marriage.

Protecting a Good Thing

God is so thoroughly pro-sex that he has established boundaries by which to protect it, to maximize its joy. He has also designed ways by which to express this spectacular gift in order to bring fulfillment. His Bible consistently and clearly establishes heterosexual monogamy—"one-flesh" marriage—as core to providing the security of enduring, growing, developing, nurtured, authentic sexual love.

This love stands in stark contrast to the throw-away, who-looks-the-best-for-the-moment type of lust that results in multiple partners and deep emotional pain and rejection.

Robert Langdon's legitimizing the antibiblical pagan under-standing of sex ultimately hurts people—badly; not just sexually, but in every aspect of their lives.

Sex is God's idea, and second to salvation, it is the best idea he ever shared with us. This is a wonderful gift God gave to us—he certainly is not ashamed of it!

CHAPTER 3
WOMEN ARE MORE SACRED AND FEMININE THAN THE "SACRED FEMININE"

"... Constantine and his male successors successfully converted the world from matriarchal paganism to patriarchal Christianity by waging a campaign of propaganda that demonized the sacred feminine, obliterating the goddess from modern religion forever" (124).

All the subtlety of *The Da Vinci Code* disappears each time the topic of women is mentioned. Brown's thesis is succinct: Christianity destroyed and killed women. Paganism affirmed them. But he is wrong. Very wrong. If ever a book should be written off as "mere fiction," *The Da Vinci Code* is the one.

On the other hand, this book can't be ignored so easily. Due to its author's effective sprinkling of occasional "facts," along with assertions by the characters that they are speaking the truth, Brown's book is neither fact nor fiction. It is "fact-ion"—that is, a wily narrative that blends limited facts with some grossly exaggerated claims (like the claim that the church killed five million women in its witch hunts); these claims are placed in the unfolding plot in real locations and times to provide sufficient plausibility. The result is a stunning and effective propaganda piece that moves its readers to a skewed perception of reality.

- Is it true that there was a matriarchal culture that the church attempted to crush?
- Is it true that the church hunted down and killed more than five million women over three centuries

as part of a brutal "reeducation" (125)?
- Is it true that the church, even today, seeks to demonize and repress women?
- Is it true that Jesus was the original feminist (248)?

Brown makes some sweeping accusations about how the church (or persons representing the church) denigrates women, treating them as accomplices of Satan. Then he creates a gender-fueled conspiracy and manipulates reality in order to demonstrate that pagan female cultures were much better than our Judeo-Christian cultures today. In doing so, Brown conveniently ignores the biblical view of women.

DID CHRISTIANITY SUBJUGATE WOMEN?

We are not saying that Brown is completely wrong in writing that women have, at times, been mistreated by those who claim to be Christians. At the same time, we object to Brown's technique of focusing on the aberrations while ignoring normative, biblically based Christianity.

As Christians, we sadly acknowledge that there are sins within the church on this issue. And those sins cannot be simply swept under the carpet. We acknowledge that the church is comprised of broken, and often sinful, people. While speaking to a large congregation, I (Jim) once asked, "Is there any man here who has not, at some time, taken advantage of a woman, or at least mistreated a woman, in some way?" No one raised his hand. We were all guilty.

The Matriarchy Myth

Brown writes, "Constantine and his male successors successfully converted the world from matriarchal paganism to patriarchal Christianity" (124). He wishfully imagines a matriarchal time before patriarchal rule.

Before we consider his claims against Christianity, let us

examine the question of patriarchal versus matriarchal in the entire scope of history. All history, including secular as well as biblical history, is more male-led than female-led. In spite of the fact that there have been many superb female leaders in both secular as well as in biblical and Christian history, the preponderance of leaders has been men.

Regarding this issue of former matriarchal societies, Steven Goldberg, chairman of the Department of Sociology at City College, City University of New York, wrote,

> The point is that authority and leadership are, and always have been, associated with the male in every society, and I refer to this when I say that patriarchy is universal and that there has never been a matriarchy.... Theories that hypothesized a matriarchal form of society at "an earlier stage of history" made a certain, if tortuous sense, until the findings of the past 50 years failed to include a single shred of evidence that such matriarchies had ever existed and demonstrated the inability of all such theories to deal with reality. [Of the h]undreds of the societies we have studied in this century ... without exception [they] have been patriarchal.... [Margaret] Mead acknowledged that "It is true ... that all the claims so glibly made about societies ruled by women are nonsense. We have no reason to believe that they ever existed."[1]

Goldberg's contentions are clear. There is not a "single shred of evidence" to show female-led early civilizations. Men, according to noted anthropologist Margaret Mead, have been in charge. These are two highly regarded scholars saying there never has been such a thing as a matriarchal society. How then, if it never existed, was Constantine able to convert it to patriarchal rule?

Which Philosophy Truly Esteems Women?

Brown implies that pagan nations affirmed women. But does that square with reality? In truth, women in the ancient pagan world were not viewed or treated as well as Langdon would have Sophie believe.

In Alvin Schmidt's groundbreaking book, *Under the Influence: How Christianity Transformed Civilization,* we see that before the coming of Christ, when the world of paganism was dominant, the lives of most women were held in very low regard. In Greece, India, and China, women had no rights and were considered the property of their husbands.

In ancient Greece, women—especially wives—were regarded as lowly. A wife was not allowed to leave her house unescorted. She was not allowed to eat or interact with guests in the home, but was consigned to her quarters (*gynaeceum*). In contrast, a *hetaera* (mistress) was allowed to accompany a married man in public.[2]

The average Athenian woman had the social status of a slave. Women were not educated, nor were they allowed to speak in public. Silence was considered the great grace of a woman, even at home. Not only were women considered inferior, they were also thought to be the source of evil and were thus not to be trusted.

The advent of Christianity radically transformed the fate of women. Even ancient Roman pagan scholars agree that it was the turning point for the freedom and dignity of women.[3]

Wherever Christianity has been introduced, it has lifted up women, not just in antiquity but even in modern times. Sex-selection infanticide was common in 1880 in pagan China before the influence of Christian missionaries. In India, the practice of suttee was ended by the influence of Christianity. A good Hindu wife was expected to follow her husband in death on the funeral pyre, even if she was young with her whole life ahead of her. "Child widows" were also part of the pagan goddess-worshipping Hindu culture. These girls were raised to be temple prostitutes. Amy Carmichael, a Christian, fought to put an end to this practice by rescuing girls from it.

THE GREAT EUROPEAN WITCH HUNT

Nevertheless, Brown paints a completely different picture through his characters in *The Da Vinci Code*. According to Professor Langdon, Christianity is violently antiwoman. Langdon recounts the atrocities of the Middle Ages, an era known as the "Great Hunt" or simply, "The Burning." Langdon recalls how the Catholic church, fueled by a publication titled *Malleus Maleficarum*, or *The Witches' Hammer*, began a crusade against any woman deemed a threat to the church's power base, labeling such a woman a witch.

> Those deemed "witches" by the Church included
> all female scholars, priestesses, gypsies, mystics,
> nature lovers, herb gatherers, and any women
> "suspiciously attuned to the natural world."
> … During three hundred years of witch hunts, the
> Church burned at the stake an astounding five
> million women (125).

Brown has based his claims on old research that has been proved unreliable and deliberately misleading. Jenny Gibbons, in an article titled "Recent Developments in the Study of The Great European Witch Hunt," writes, "Many articles in Pagan magazines contain almost no accurate information about the 'Burning Times,' primarily because we rely so heavily on outdated research."[4]

For instance, Brown refers to *Malleus Maleficarum* as being authored by an official of the Catholic church. Actually, the church reacted to its publication by rejecting the legal procedures suggested by the authors and censuring them a few years later. It was secular courts, not the church, that relied on

Malleus Maleficarum and handed down the majority of capital sentences. Those found guilty of witchcraft by the church were usually given nonlethal penalties.

Gibbons continues: "Today, we know that there is absolutely no evidence to support this theory. When the church was at the height of its power (11th to 14th centuries) very few witches died. Persecutions did not reach epidemic levels until after the Reformation, when the Catholic church had lost its position as Europe's indisputable moral authority."[5]

It was Christian missionaries who encouraged kingdoms and courts to pass laws protecting men and women from charges of witchcraft. These missionaries said such charges were ungrounded, as they did not believe humans possessed the power to do what witches were accused of doing.

And what of the estimates of the number of women killed during the Great Hunt? The estimated number of those killed ranges from hundreds of thousands to nine million. Brown uses the figure of five million. But again, modern research reveals that this is not the case.

"On the wilder shores of the feminist and witch-cult movements," writes Robin Briggs, a scholar at Oxford University, "a potent myth has become established, to the effect that nine million women were burned as witches in Europe; gendercide rather than genocide. This is an over-estimate by a factor of up to 200, for most reasonable modern estimates suggest perhaps 100,000 trials between 1450 and 1750, with something between 40,000 and 50,000 executions, of which 20 to 25 percent were men."[6]

Even so, scholars Ross Clifford and Philip Johnson aptly voice the sentiment of most biblically consistent Christians: "That was 40,000 casualties too many … the Inquisition and Salem trials were a hideous violation of human dignity and utterly inexcusable."[7] Indeed, while the number of so-called witches burned has been wildly exaggerated, Christians must concede that the burning of even one person is indefensible.

Gibbons concludes her essay by saying, "We Neopagans now face a crisis. As new data appeared, historians altered their theories to account for it. We have not. Therefore an enormous gap has opened between the academic and the 'average' Pagan view of witchcraft.... We avoid the somewhat dull academic texts that present solid research, preferring sensational writers who play to our emotions."[8]

Gibbons wrote this in 1998, nearly five years before the publication of *The Da Vinci Code*. She is a self-confessed pagan who is concerned about writers using misleading information to cast the church in a negative light in reference to the Great Hunt.

THE TRUTH ABOUT
THE BIBLE'S ESTEEM OF WOMEN

If Dan Brown had wanted to use reliable information for his research into how Christians view women, he need not have gone any further than the Bible. Consider the examples from the Old Testament.

In Genesis, we learn that both males and females receive their identity, their sense of value, from their relationship with the Creator, being made in the image of God (1:27).

The Da Vinci Code repeatedly misquotes the Bible, stating that Eve ate the fruit; thus she, the first female, brought sin into the world. However, in Genesis 2, which provides more detail regarding creation than Genesis 1, the instruction not to eat the fruit was given to the male, Adam, before the female was created (Genesis 2:16–18, 22). The primary disobedience in Genesis 3 was the failure of the male to give protection, leadership, and nurture to his home. This was not merely a woman's sin. This was, first of all, a man's sin. Cowardly Adam tries to shift the blame to Eve ("the woman," Genesis 3:12) and even to God ("you put here with me," Genesis 3:12).

Eve was an accomplice. That is why God confronts both of them (Genesis 3:9–19).

The apostle Paul states it even more emphatically. He says that sin entered the world through the actions of one man, Adam (Romans 5:17).

Exalted Women of the Old Testament

Consider more examples of how women are portrayed in the Old Testament.

- Esther was courageous to the point of defying the king himself, an action that usually resulted in death. The outcome of her courage was the salvation of an entire race of people (Esther 1–10).
- Ruth was loyal, astute, and shrewd. She humbled herself in order to secure food for herself and her mother-in-law. And she was obedient, marrying a stranger who ended up loving and caring for Ruth and her family (Ruth 1–4).
- Deborah was a wife, mother, and judge in Israel (Judges 4).

Proverbs 31 affirms the greatness of women, demonstrating their ability to juggle the amazing pressures as community leaders, businesswomen, wives, and mothers. The chapter exalts the qualities of one whom the Bible portrays as a model woman:

- She is skilled with her hands (vv. 13, 19) and her mind (vv. 13–31).
- She understands manufacturing (vv. 13, 24); importing (v. 14); time management (v. 15); real estate investing (v. 16); agribusiness (v. 16); physical workouts (v. 17); business profit (vv. 16, 18, 24); a work ethic (vv. 15, 18); "hands-on" labor (v. 19); welfare and compassion (v. 20); planning, administration, and organization (v. 21); and fashion (vv. 21–22).

- When she speaks, she is articulate and her speech is content-rich (v. 26).
- She is an instructor, a teacher (v. 26).
- She is an unashamed homemaker—and a good one (v. 27).
- Not surprisingly, she is busy—very busy (v. 27).
- She enjoys being a mother and is quite successful in child rearing (v. 28).

Does this sound like a repressed woman?

Exalted Women of the New Testament

The New Testament begins with "the genealogy of Jesus Christ" (Matthew 1:1–16). The fictional Robert Langdon insists the New Testament was manipulated into being by a group of female-bashing chauvinists. If that is so, then why would these male elitists allow women to have a prominent role in the genealogy, a most unusual inclusion considering that a typical lineage at that time would have included only males? If the early leaders of Christianity were as villainous as *The Da Vinci Code* states, then no women would have been included. But five were. Who were these five women?

- Tamar—a twice-widowed woman who had sexual relations with her father-in-law—was the first woman to be mentioned (Genesis 38:11–30).
- Rahab was a prostitute in the city of Jericho (Joshua 2:1).
- Ruth was a woman with a sterling character (Ruth 2:11).
- The wife of Uriah, Bathsheba, is remembered as the woman with whom King David had an affair (2 Samuel 11:1–27).
- The final woman in the genealogy of Christ is, predictably, Mary, the mother of Jesus (Matthew 1:16). Presumably between the ages of thirteen and fifteen,

in a small community, Mary became pregnant—
before marriage and, miraculously, without having
had sexual intercourse. The role of the mother was so
honored as to be cited in a list that would typically
include only the father.

And the examples don't stop with Mary, Jesus' mother.
Jesus' very first announcement that he was the Messiah was
shared with a woman, and not just any woman. She was a
five-time divorcee, involved with a live-in boyfriend.
Furthermore, she was a Samaritan, which meant that Jesus
violated the mores of the time by crossing racial lines (John
4:17–26).

When Mary (the sister of Martha and Lazarus) listened
to Jesus' teachings (at that time an activity reserved for males)
and Martha scurried about fulfilling the "female" role, Jesus
affirmed Mary and challenged Martha (Luke 10:41–42).

In contrast to the custom of the time, a group of women
were part of the entourage that traveled with Jesus and other
men. These women even supported his ministry financially
(Luke 8:1–3).

In the book of Acts, Peter cites an Old Testament scripture saying that both "your sons and daughters will
prophesy" (Joel 2:28).

Paul, who is so often accused by feminists of being antiwoman, uses forceful language to declare that both sexes
have equal standing before Christ. Neither males nor females
have precedent in God's eyes (Galatians 3:28).

The single strongest affirmation of women in the New
Testament is found in the fact that a woman—who, according
to the customs of the time, would not have been allowed to
testify in court—is the one to testify regarding the single most
important announcement in all of biblical or Christian history:
the actual, literal, physical resurrection of Jesus from the dead
(Matthew 28:1; Mark 16:1; Luke 24:10).

In light of the evidence cited above, we submit that anyone who claims the Holy Bible is intended to repress women has not read the Bible very carefully. On the contrary, it tells us that God holds women in high esteem, and thus, so should Christians everywhere.

Women in the Early Church

Brown also asserts, "[P]owerful men in the early Christian church 'conned' the world by propagating lies that devalued the female and tipped the scales in favor of the masculine" (124). Is this true?

While the Bible itself, and Jesus personally, upheld a high respect for women, it must be acknowledged that there were antiwomen statements from church leaders—Tertullian, Cyril of Jerusalem, Jerome, and Augustine as examples—during the third through fifth centuries. Some of these continued through persons such as Thomas Aquinas and others, even past the Reformation. Such statements are contrary to the Bible and to Jesus. Those statements are an embarrassment to all Christians.

Thankfully, those statements are offset by volumes of strong affirmations of women, and by the massive number of females who have ministered so effectively throughout the centuries of Christianity. The writings of the early church fathers can be taken affirmatively or negatively, depending upon what one wishes to extract.

Admittedly, other writers of this age were less affirming. Some early writings blamed women for the inability of men to control their sexual desires. Other writers even insisted that women should confine themselves to childbearing and maintenance of the home. To deny the existence of this stream of thought would be less than honest.

However, present-day radical feminism has been obsessed with such statements, aggrandizing them and developing an entire feminist theology that insists early Christianity was fundamentally misogynistic. Using such venomous language to describe early Christianity, as a whole, is a broad generalization to say the least, and historically dishonest. *The Da Vinci Code* perpetrates this inaccurate and misleading "woman-hating" claim.

Brown seems unaware of the spectacular contributions of innumerable women throughout church history. These women were strong. They were leaders. They were respected. And they were all part of the inexpressible contribution of women in Christian history.

But if Robert Langdon is correct, then there would be no record of women in the church's history. Women in the ministry, if the premise of *The Da Vinci Code* is correct, would have disappeared because of the oppression of "Constantine and his male successors."

The hard but significant question is this: If Brown is correct, if the church has set out to systematically demonize the role of women in ministry, how do we account for all the great women throughout history, and in our lifetime, who have had such an incredible impact in the spiritual welfare of so many others?

Was Jesus the First Feminist?

Christianity, as we have seen, strongly upholds women. The church, while fallible, has also taken great steps to protect and esteem women. So why are Christians and the church cast as antifeminist?

The first women's rights conference in America was held in a Wesleyan church in 1848 in Seneca Falls, New York. On the 150th anniversary of this event, in 1998, there was a celebration of this conference. Yet in the national media coverage of that event, there was no mention of the church's role in the first conference. Perhaps that was because early feminism was biblical feminism based on the scriptural understanding of women: It is unrelated to today's radical pagan feminism.

Ironically, Brown's character Leigh Teabing was partially correct when he said, "Jesus was the original feminist" (248). Jesus, as we showed earlier, validated the role and value of women. Brown, however, recasts Jesus as a worshipper of Robert Langdon's paganistic "sacred feminine," a mockery of all recognized and credible research.

Jesus as the first feminist? Yes, if that means Jesus was always for the outcast, the forsaken, the mistreated, the hopeless. It was Jesus, not the pagan world that surrounded him, who began to turn the tide in the way women are to be treated. By treating women as equals, Jesus also criticized the evil of male chauvinism. And the same must be said of the apostles who followed him.

There is, however, one more thing we need to say. Jesus also knew that God the Creator, as the crowning of his work, created males and females to be different. This is the beautiful balance that the Bible seeks to maintain, which Jesus maintained—males and females gloriously different but unquestionably equal.

Chauvinism Is Not Honorable

When Robin Morgan—the first radical feminist I (Jim) ever heard speak—came to Princeton Theological Seminary when I was a student there in the 1970s, she purposely ignored all males who raised their hands during the question-and-answer time. This, according to her, was so that "the sisterhood could experience power." This is the same woman who stated, "I feel that 'man-hating' is honorable."[9]

No, "man-hating" is not honorable. It is wrong. So is woman-hating. Chauvinism is wrong, whether it comes from men or from women. Women taking advantage of men are no better than men taking advantage of women. Both are wrong. Both are unbiblical. Both are un-Christian. *The Da Vinci Code* drives the gender wedge deeper, uplifting women at the expense of men, which is as offensive as uplifting men at the expense of women.

Brown brings out the worst in all of us with Sophie's innocent question, "You're saying the Christian church was to be carried on by a woman?" (248). No, the Christian church was not to be carried on by a woman. It is to be carried on by both men and women—persons, not separated by the culturally imposed restrictions of being male or female, but who instead embrace Jesus Christ (Galatians 3:28). The church was not and is not a "man's thing." Nor is it a "woman's thing." It is to be carried on by the people who follow God.

Contrary to *The Da Vinci Code*, the Bible, in particular, and Christianity, in general, are not antiwoman. In contrast, *The Da Vinci Code* expresses implicit and explicit antimale sentiments.

What is driving Dan Brown's agenda? It is the pagan worldview that denies and distorts a core biblical truth: Men and women are created equal but different.

CHAPTER 4
JESUS—WHO WAS HE, REALLY?

"Many scholars claim that the early Church literally stole Jesus from His original followers, hijacking His human message, shrouding it in an impenetrable cloak of divinity, and using it to expand their own power" (233).

Just who was Jesus?

The answer to this question will not only shape the way you view *The Da Vinci Code*, but will ultimately shape your entire life. For, if Brown is correct in saying that Jesus was just a man, then our further debate with the author is meaningless. But if there is more to Jesus than Brown asserts, if Jesus truly is divine (with no help from Emperor Constantine), then we must also accept that what Jesus taught about life and eternity is true. Everything hangs on the answer to this question.

- Is it true that Jesus' divinity was the result of a vote of bishops (233)?
- Is it true that the early church hijacked Jesus' message and shrouded it with divinity (233)?
- Is it true that Jesus was simply "a mortal prophet … a great and powerful man, but a man nonetheless. A mortal" (233)?

LIFE'S PIVOTAL QUESTION

Why were the followers of Jesus during his time on this earth so sure he was really divine? At what point did they come to that conclusion? On one occasion, Jesus asked his closest companions, "Who do you say I am?" (Matthew 16:13–20). This is a key moment in the life of Jesus. In contemporary language, the scene may have looked like this:

Jesus gathered his followers around him one day and said, "Hey, guys."

"Yes?" the disciples responded.

"You read the *Jerusalem Times'* op-ed piece, along with the letters to the editor. Who do they think I am?"

"Well, Jesus," one of them began, "some say that since you shed tears when you speak, you are old Jeremiah come back to life."

Another one chimed in, "Yes, but others think that since you have done so many miracles, you are really Elijah come back to life."

"There's another theory floating around about you," another one stated, interrupting the previous disciple.

"And what is that?" Jesus asked.

"Well, since you preach really straight and direct, others think you are one of the prophet-preachers from seven hundred years ago come back to life."

"Very interesting," Jesus mused. "But what I really want to know is this: Who do you guys think I am?" It got quiet. Jesus had never put them on the spot like this before.

Peter spoke up first—as he often did. But this time he did not embarrass his friends. In fact, the blustery Peter was a bit low key. He started hesitatingly. "I know who you are!"

"Who?" Jesus asked gently.

"You are ..." Peter paused, then slowly completed the sentence, his confidence building, "... the Christ—the Messiah, the actual Son of God himself!"

There was a long silence. Jesus stared intently at Peter, then at each of the other eleven close friends with him that day. They all knew the history of people claiming to be messiahs. During the four hundred years between the close of the Old Testament and the beginning of the New Testament, there were numerous individuals who claimed that they were the messiah. Each new messiah had raised the hopes of those who believed him. Then he had faded away. And with that supposed messiah went many broken hopes and dreams. So, was Jesus just another one? Would he disappear like all the rest?

After what seemed like a very long time, he finally spoke. "You're right, Peter. But you could not have learned that truth only from studying and reading the Old Testament. God, my Father, told you that in a direct, inspired way so that your words would be the rock of my church, declaring to the world who I really am."

He paused much longer this time. "So now," he said, "the word is out. You know who I am. And on that truth, on the reality that I am the Christ, the Messiah—the Son of the Living God—I am going to launch an unstoppable force. It will be called the church. It will be stronger than hell itself. But I must ask for a favor." His words just hung there. He didn't say anything more for a moment.

"Yes?" one of his friends said, wanting to break the silence.

"Do not tell anyone—at least not yet—that I am God, that I am Christ, that I am Messiah. Not yet."

What does Brown do with this conversation Jesus had with his disciples? What does he do with this rock upon which the church has been built for two thousand years? How does he respond to this essential truth today's followers of Christ hold most dear?

MERE MORTAL, OR MESSIAH?

Perhaps you are one of those readers who have been impressed by *The Da Vinci Code*'s case against biblical Christianity. Indeed, one must admit that if Jesus truly was merely a mortal man, and if this conversation we just read is false, then the heart is ripped out of the good news of Christianity and the Bible is not worth the paper it's written on.

But since we need all the good news we can get, we

should hesitate before throwing out the good news of the Christian message, unless, of course, we have solid grounds for doing so. Answering *The Da Vinci Code*'s severe charge demands patience. Such a breathtaking, far-reaching generalization about Jesus will require responses in a number of following chapters, so stay with us and read on.

Let's begin by examining Brown's major assertion that "The early Church literally stole Jesus from His original followers, hijacking His human message, shrouding it in an impenetrable cloak of divinity ... to expand their own power" (233).

To make sense of this claim we need to ask:

1. Who were "the original followers" that Brown names?
2. Where can we find this original "human message," and what is its content?
3. Who was part of "the early Church" who stole Jesus from these early followers?
4. When was this message distorted?
5. When was Jesus "shrouded in divinity"?

The Original "Gnostic" Followers

The Da Vinci Code makes a great deal of the discovery in 1945 of "secret scrolls," the so-called Nag Hammadi Gnostic texts. For the moment, it is sufficient to know that Brown, following a marginal group of scholars who are committed to the undermining of biblical Christianity (particularly a group called the Jesus Seminar), argues that the "original disciples" were a group called Gnostics, not the writers of our New Testament.

Who were these Gnostics? In a nutshell, Gnostics were people who believed that every Christian was a "christ," and thus every Christian was "divine." Jesus was thus christ and divine only in this sense, not in any unique sense. Brown contends these Gnostic "original disciples" came before the men we associate as Jesus' disciples—Peter, James, John, and the rest. In order for Brown's theory to work, Peter and the rest of the New Testament disciples must have twisted the writings of the allegedly original Gnostic disciples.

The Original Human Message

Their so-called human message is supposedly contained in one of these Gnostic texts called the Gospel of Thomas, as well as in a hypothetical document no one has ever seen called "Q." Both of these are claimed to predate the Gospels of the New Testament. In neither of these documents is there any teaching on the death, physical resurrection, and divine nature of Jesus, so Jesus is interpreted to be a human, though very spiritual, "guru" like the Buddha, concerned only with justice in this world. Are these documents reliable? We shall see.

Who Was in Brown's Early Church?

The later "early Church," according to Brown's theory, is made up of the apostles we all know—including Peter, John, Matthew, and Paul—who wrote the New Testament, imposing their later version of things on the original, human, Gnostic Jesus. From these apostles we get the "orthodox" Jesus, who died for the sins of the world, who rose from the dead, who left behind him an empty tomb, and who was God in flesh. Gnostics say this version of Jesus is a fabrication.

According to modern scholars who hold to the Gnostic worldview, the alleged fabrication clearly took place when the "orthodox" Christians mentioned above wrote down their beliefs about Jesus in the biblical Gospels, suppressing the original texts and the true story of Jesus, specifically by making him divine. This special sense of the term *divine*, as used by the church, meant that Jesus was the unique mediator between the transcendent divine Creator and sinful humanity—according to *The Da Vinci Code*, a lie.

We will explore these and related topics in subsequent chapters; but even before we explore these topics in depth, we can see that Brown's explanation of the events of early Christianity runs out of time.

TIMING IS EVERYTHING

Our earliest Christian writings come from the pen of the apostle Paul, who wrote from around AD 48 to around AD 60. All recognized scholars and historians support this fact.[1] They agree Paul was a historical figure, a contemporary of Jesus, who, as a convinced rabbi, knew the early Christians well enough that he at first sought their extinction. In the late thirties he converted to Christianity, became a recognized Christian apostle, and finally was executed for his faith by Nero in AD 66. There is no fact of early Christianity more historically verified and generally accepted by foes and friends alike.

What is more, Paul's writings constitute the backbone of the New Testament. Since the life and ministry of Paul overlaps the historical beginnings of the Christian movement, he is the most historically dependable window into the faith of the earliest disciples of Jesus.

What scholars, such as those from the Jesus Seminar, and storytellers, such as Dan Brown, would have us believe is this: The "original Gnostic disciples" believed in a mortal (nondeity) Jesus. These disciples wrote their "gospels" portraying Jesus as a good man, a moral teacher, but not as divine. But these disciples somehow lost control of "their" Jesus to a group who took over (Brown uses the dramatic term "hijack[ed]") this growing sect called Christianity and completely reinterpreted the life, message, and mission of Jesus. This original group of Gnostics then disappeared without a trace until the middle of the second century.

Yet somehow, Paul, a prolific writer about Jesus and the church, never made mention of these "original Gnostic believers." The Gnostic argument is not serious history; it is a piece of fiction that cannot be substantiated.

The unimpeachable historicity of the apostle Paul and his writings completely undermines *The Da Vinci Code*'s view of things. Paul said that he depended on those who were apostles before him, and specifically named Peter, John, and James, Jesus' brother (1 Corinthians 9:5; Galatians 1:19; 2:8–9). He actually said, around AD 50, that he received from these men the original gospel (1 Corinthians 15:3–5), again mentioning Peter and actually citing a text that came from the thirties that emphasized the absolute importance of Jesus' death and resurrection.[2] He called these men "pillars" (Galatians 2:9), that is, the foundational, eyewitness figures (1 Corinthians 15:5) on whom Jesus built the church (Matthew 16:15–18; Ephesians 2:20).

If any historical person was in a position to identify what the original faith of the church was and what the original founders believed about Jesus, it was Paul. Paul said that what he preached was what these original founders preached (1 Corinthians 15:11).

In other words, what Paul preached was what the earliest church believed. As soon as we can nail down what Paul said about Jesus, we will know what the true original disciples believed about Jesus—which is not dependent on speculative theories but on solid history.

Shrouded in Divinity

When was Jesus shrouded in divinity? The simple answer is, from the beginning. The earliest disciples, as Paul shows, believed and taught that Jesus was a man, born from a human mother (Galatians 4:4). But in the same verse he called Jesus God's Son in the absolute sense of having a divine nature. Lest there be any doubt, Paul actually described Jesus as "being in very nature God" (Philippians 2:6). He wrote this early in the fifties. What is more, he cited a kind of hymn that is very Jewish and which doubtless goes back to the apostles in Palestine in the earliest days of the church (Philippians 2:5–11).

Add to these two texts from the earliest days of the church the mature statements of Paul about the divinity of Jesus—texts such as Romans 1:3 ("his [God's] Son"), 1 Corinthians 8:6 ("one Lord, Jesus Christ, through whom all things came"), and Colossians 1:15–16 ("He [Christ] is the image of the invisible God … by him all things were created"), and it is clear that the fourth century did not invent the divinity of Jesus. The church in its earliest days held strongly to the belief that Jesus was completely and wholly divine in nature.

HOW DID JESUS VIEW HIMSELF?

If Paul is right, the Gospels are the earliest record of Jesus' earthly life. Paul knew Peter, James, and John, along with the other apostles, who were the earliest followers of Jesus and eyewitnesses to what Jesus said. He testifies that their witness was the true and authentic one. Their Gospels contain Jesus' teachings about himself. What did Jesus teach his disciples concerning himself? Here are just a handful of his claims to divinity.

- He allowed others to call him the Christ (Matthew 16:15–20; 26:63–64).
- He said he could forgive sin (Matthew 9:2–6; Luke 7:47–48).
- He did not stop others from calling him the Son of God (Matthew 14:33).
- He promised to rise from the dead (Matthew 20:18–19; 27:62–63).

- He said He would be the ultimate judge at the end of time (Matthew 25:31–46).

WOULD YOU DIE FOR A LIE?

Those who saw *The Passion of the Christ*, the incredibly moving film directed by Mel Gibson, will recall the horrific torture that Jesus endured before his death. The cruelty was extreme, even to the Romans who were masters of extreme cruelty. Why would a "good" man endure such punishment? If Jesus did not believe himself to be divine, why did he not confess his deception and avoid such agony?

Those who followed Jesus in life also followed him in death. These, too, could have avoided needless suffering had they but declared that Jesus was just a man. But they did not. According to oral traditions passed down from the early church, here is how some of Jesus' disciples met their end:

- James the son of Zebedee was beheaded.
- Simon Peter was crucified in Rome. It is said that, at his request, he was crucified upside down, saying, "I am not worthy to die in the manner of Jesus."
- Paul was beheaded by Nero in AD 66.
- Stephen was stoned by a mob in AD 38.

These are but a few of the martyrs who did not deny Jesus' divinity. If Jesus' followers did not hold him to be the Son of God, if that truly was a fourth-century invention, all these men died for no reason at all.

SUDDENLY DIVINE?

Let's return to *The Da Vinci Code*'s assertion that Jesus was not considered divine until the year AD 325, when Constantine, for political purposes, manipulated some bishops to "vote" Jesus divine. In addition to evidence from Paul and the writings of the early church, there are many more confirmations of the divinity of Jesus. All of these demonstrate that long before the Council of Nicæa, the leaders of the church considered Jesus divine. Here is what several of these leaders wrote (years approximate):

- Ignatius: "God himself was manifested in human form" (AD 105).
- Clement: "It is fitting that you should think of Jesus Christ as of God" (AD 150).
- Justin Martyr: "The Father of the universe has a Son. And he … is even God" (AD 160).
- Irenaeus: "He is God, for the name Emmanuel indicates this" (AD 180).
- Tertullian: "… Christ our God" (AD 200).
- Origen: "No one should be offended that the Savior is also God …" (AD 225).
- Novatian: "… He is not only man, but God also …" (AD 235).
- Cyprian: "Jesus Christ, our Lord and God" (AD 250).
- Methodius: "… He truly was and is … with God, and being God …" (AD 290).
- Lactantius: "We believe him to be God" (AD 304).
- Arnobius: "Christ performed all those miracles … the … duty of Divinity" (AD 305).[3]

WHAT REALLY HAPPENED AT NICÆA?

Brown's character, Teabing, warms to the subject of the Nicæan Council while teaching Sophie about Jesus:

"Jesus' establishment as the 'Son of God' was officially proposed and voted on by the Council of Nicæa."

"Hold on. You're saying Jesus' divinity was the result of a vote?"

"A relatively close vote at that," Teabing added (233).

Councils held to determine important doctrinal matters were not uncommon to the early Christians. We read in Acts 15 how the church leaders came together to decide how Gentiles were to be treated. Councils were important in order to maintain an orthodox faith and prevent the spread of false teaching.

One such false teaching was being spread by Arius in AD 318. Arius taught that Jesus was a created being, just like other humans, and not the "begotten Son of God." He was opposed by Alexander, the bishop of Alexandria, who declared Arius a heretic in a local council in AD 321. So Arius moved to Palestine and continued his teaching there. If he had kept his ideas to his own followers, there would not have been cause to call a council. But Arius began sending letters to area churches promoting the idea of Jesus as a created being. The debate grew over the next few years, finally gaining the attention of the emperor, Constantine.

Constantine, who had consolidated his hold on the Roman Empire, sought unity in all regions. He knew that a division within the Christian church would be one more destabilizing force in the empire, so he moved to restore peace. Constantine called together more than three hundred bishops from around the empire, primarily from the east. (This would have favored Arius's cause, as that is where his influence was greatest.) Bishops traveled thousands of miles to attend the conference held in Constantinople. Many came bearing wounds and scars from torture they had endured for their faith.

The Arians submitted their statement of doctrine that flatly denied the divinity of Christ. It was soundly rejected. The bishops, led by Athanasius, considered what was taught by the original church in the writings of the New Testament. These men wrote up an alternative creed, which became the blueprint for the Nicene Creed. In it Jesus was affirmed to be divine, the historic position of the church for the previous three hundred years.

The new creed was adopted. Only two voted against. That can hardly be called a close vote. The church had suffered for three centuries under the tyranny of the Roman Empire. The Council of Nicæa came only fourteen years after the final persecution of Christians at the hands of Emperor Galerius. The bishops of the church would never have compromised what had cost their fellow Christians so much. They would have rather suffered another three centuries of oppression and persecution than deny their Lord.

Yet *The Da Vinci Code* makes this, one of the most sublime theological legacies of the ancient church, appear to be mere political propaganda. Even if Constantine's motives were not driven by his desire for correct doctrine—which no one knows—it doesn't matter. The evidence of history and the light of Scripture affirm the divinity of Christ. The apostles, the persecuted church, and the Nicene bishops did not revise history, they affirmed it. For them it certainly was not "the greatest story ever sold." Many paid for their faith with their own blood.

CHAPTER 5
WHO IS REVISING HISTORY?

*... the Church had a deceitful and violent history. Their brutal
crusade to "reeducate" the pagan and feminine-worshipping
religions spanned three centuries (124).*

There are hidden documents that prove the Bible's account
of Jesus' life is false. These documents, if found and
revealed, would show Jesus as a mortal who never rose from
the dead. They would prove that Jesus and Mary Magdalene
were married and had children together. They could point to
persons alive today who are descendants of Jesus and Mary.
And it is these secret documents, according to *The Da Vinci
Code*, that hold the true historical records—not the Bible and
the writings of the church fathers.

- Is it true that the church has rewritten history to
  present a one-sided account of the faith (233–235)?
- Is it true that the church has suppressed knowledge
  about a marriage between Jesus and Mary
  Magdalene that, if known, would destroy
  Christianity (244, 249)?
- Is it true that the church knows the whereabouts of
  the Holy Grail but has committed murder and
  employed "horrific" methods to keep this knowledge
  hidden (266)?

DID THE CHURCH REWRITE HISTORY?

Leigh Teabing, the famous historian in *The Da Vinci Code*,
gives us a lesson in the making of historical records:

"[H]istory is always written by the winners. When two cultures clash, the loser is obliterated, and the winner writes the history books—books which glorify their own cause and disparage the conquered foe. As Napoleon once said, 'What is history, but a fable agreed upon?'" (256).

Who are we to believe? Dan Brown, through his characters, discounts the Bible with one sweep of his pen. He says that winners write history, implying that since Christians were the winners in the power struggle during the time of Constantine, they were able to rewrite history to their advantage. They staged a "fable agreed upon." The fable? That Jesus was a divine being who, after dying, rose from the dead. This, according to Teabing and Langdon, is not provable, so it must be a falsehood written by "winners."

In order to accept this theory as presented in *The Da Vinci Code*, we must deal with facts that cannot be disputed. We will look in detail at the assembly of our Bible in the next chapter. But for now, consider this point: A number of scholars make an excellent case that the New Testament books were all written before AD 70. At that time, as we discussed earlier, Christians were a minority, persecuted by both fellow Jews and the Romans. They could not, in any way, be considered "winners" when these books were written. They were killed for maintaining their faith when a simple verbal rejection of Jesus would have saved them from a cruel death. These are the ones Brown considers "winners"?

The Biblical Account: Warts and All

If the writers of the Bible were trying to manipulate history in their favor, why would they include so many accounts of the failures of their "star players"? For instance, the Bible clearly records the accounts of David covering up his affair with a married woman by having her husband killed (2 Samuel 11), or

Peter being impetuous and frequently saying and doing foolish things (Matthew 16:22–23; 17:1–5; 26:33–34, 69–75).

If the pages of the Bible had been tampered with or rewritten to make its cause look good, these and many other stories would have been deleted. In their place would be stories of how these people were perfect in every way.

For that matter, if Christians truly were the "winners" who could rewrite history in their favor, why did they include in their list of church leaders men and women who were less than perfect? Yet history recounts case after case of revered men and women of faith who were nevertheless flawed, or even corrupt.

The church doesn't have to rewrite history to hide anything. The church, as someone has said, "is not a museum of saints, but a laboratory for sinners." People frequently fail in their desire to emulate Christ, and writers of church history— the inspired writers of the Bible as well as past and present-day writers—are known for exposing, rather than trying to cover up, any of the blemishes of the church's very long story. If *The Da Vinci Code*'s thesis is correct that the church rewrites history, then we would not know all the stories of the failures of those who were part of the long history of the church.

THE "NOMINAL" CHURCH

Brown uses the term "Church" (with a capital C) throughout *The Da Vinci Code* synonymously with "Rome." (See page 266 of *The Da Vinci Code* for an example.) For both terms he is referring to the Roman Catholic Church. Since he spends much time going back and forth in the history of the early church, we feel it is important to slow down and look more closely at the formation of the church. This will reveal many of the significant points that *The Da Vinci Code* fails to tell.

From AD 100 until around AD 300, Christians remained

a minority. At first they were, for the most part, tolerated or ignored by the Roman government. But as their influence increased, so did the persecution.

Roman emperor Nero ordered the beheading of Paul and the crucifixion of Peter in AD 64. But it was not until the second century that Christianity was officially outlawed. Persecution was sporadic until the third century when Roman officials, trying to calm an increasingly panicked public, began widespread persecution of Christians. The people blamed the numerous barbaric invasions on these believers who held to their claim that there is only one God, thus showing disrespect to the pagan Roman gods.

The persecutions reached a crescendo at the beginning of the fourth century under coemperors Diocletian and Galerius, who removed all Christians from places of influence in the government and military, burned churches, and tortured and killed Christians in the public arenas. Yet, through all of these violent acts perpetrated against the church, believers in Christ continued to increase in numbers faster than they could be killed. Clearly, those who chose to be identified as Christians did so because of their firm belief in Jesus and his radical teachings. At that point in history, there was no rational reason to be known as a follower of the Christ. Again, these were not winners rewriting history.

Compromise, Not Conversion

In AD 312, Constantine was proclaimed emperor of the West. He credited the Christian God with helping him to win the military battles that led to this proclamation. In AD 313, he met with the emperor of the East in Milan, where they both declared tolerance toward all religions, especially Christianity. While on the surface this event would seem to be a major victory for the faith, it was almost its undoing.

Constantine set out to form a union between the

Christian church and the Roman Empire. He gave land and money to the churches to rebuild what previous emperors had destroyed. The church began to depend on the Roman government for money not only to finance its buildings, but also to pay its leaders.

By AD 380, Christianity was the officially established religion of the entire Roman Empire. This declaration resulted, not in authentic conversion by which people willingly and knowingly embraced Christianity, but in a redefinition of what it meant to be a Christian, thus compromising authentic Christianity. Thousands simply declared themselves (or were forced to declare themselves) to be Christian, with no understanding of what that declaration meant. Brown's character Robert Langdon has it wrong. Rather than Christianity crushing paganism, the paganistic influence within the church caused great confusion among the believers.

This huge influx of pagans, now calling themselves Christians, created what we are calling the "nominal" ("in name only") church. The church that *The Da Vinci Code* generally presents is this nominal church, made up of people who called themselves "Christian" but who had no idea what the term meant.

The "Real" Church

True believers were aghast at what they saw happening. This was a group of people—many of whom still bore scars from torture endured at the hands of the Romans—who believed in the living Christ enough that they were willing to suffer and die. These were men and women who, though they loved their pagan neighbors and wanted to see them converted, had no desire to embrace their gods. We will call this group the "real" church.

The real church was begun by Christ. It is first mentioned

by Jesus in Matthew 16:18 in a discussion with Peter. But the most profound description of the church occurs in the second chapter of the book of Acts (2:42–47) in the New Testament—on the day that the church actually began. The real church consists of those who authentically embrace Christ as the one who forgives their sins and who is to be Lord, directing their lives.

What Is a "Christian"?

If we raise the question regarding what a church is, that raises the question of what a "Christian" really is. Some people say, "I am a Christian." What they really mean by that is that they are not a Muslim, or a Jew, or a Buddhist, or a Hindu. But that does not make them a Christian. You are not a Christian simply because you are not a part of other religions. You are a Christian only to the extent that you are a follower of Christ as Savior and Lord. Simply saying you are a Christian doesn't make you a Christian. Simply saying you are part of the real church doesn't make you part of the real church.

There are people who say they are a part of the church, but when you spend a little bit of time with them you find out quickly they do not embrace Jesus Christ as Lord and Savior, and they do not follow the teachings of the Bible. Therefore, just saying you're part of the church does not make you part of the church.

Would the Real Church Please Stand Up?

The Da Vinci Code often selects some of the things that people did in the name of the church that are not representative of the true church. By focusing on these activities, it condemns all of Christianity. Is *The Da Vinci Code* correct that "the Church" abused people? The answer is both yes and no. It depends on which church is being referred to. The nominal church does not look to Christ as being fully sufficient for salvation, nor is it concerned with adherence to the Bible.

Thus it has, most certainly, abused many. And it consistently violates the Bible. An obvious example is the Roman Catholic Inquisition in the Middle Ages, in which people were tortured and killed if they deviated from the dogma and structure of the church at that time.

The point is this: There is much about the church of the Middle Ages that is inexcusable. No one can defend it. No one should. At the same time, the true church of the time was comprised of many spectacular Christians who reflected Jesus Christ powerfully and who were also part of the Roman Catholic Church. Thus when Brown says "the Church," he sloppily includes the *true* church of the Middle Ages. This might make an engaging novel. But it is a distortion of history.

JESUS AND MARY MAGDALENE

The next question we need to answer deals with the relationship between Jesus and Mary Magdalene. Brown wants us to believe that the church has, throughout history, conducted a "smear campaign" to malign the character of Mary Magdalene. It is, according to Brown, part of the church's overall effort to remove the "goddess" from our worship. He shows this through a bizarre speculation into da Vinci's *Last Supper* fresco, as well as wrong teachings about the church's portrayal of Mary Magdalene.

Langdon and Teabing are teaching Sophie Neveu about the Holy Grail as they examine a reproduction of da Vinci's *Last Supper* in a book:

> Sophie scanned the work eagerly. "Does this fresco tell us what the Grail really is?"
>
> "Not what it is," Teabing whispered. "But rather who it is. The Holy Grail is not a thing. It is, in fact, a … person" (236).

Langdon and Teabing go on to explain to Sophie how da

Vinci, in his famous fresco, allegedly depicted Mary Magdalene as one of the disciples. From this, and other sources they quote, they deduce that Mary was Jesus' companion ("the word companion, in those days, literally meant spouse," says Teabing [246]) and the two had a child together. Thus, from this hypothesis it is presented that Mary herself is the Holy Grail, the recipient of the seed of Jesus. From this scenario, Brown weaves his code—the return of goddess worship into our culture.

Earlier, Professor Langdon tellingly contemplates: "A career hazard of symbologists was a tendency to extract hidden meaning from situations that had none" (171–172). Unintentionally, this statement aptly describes the fantasies of *The Da Vinci Code* with regard to Mary Magdalene. Teabing explains to Sophia Neveu, "The Church needed to defame Mary Magdalene in order to cover up her dangerous secret— her role as the Holy Grail." (244). Thus, the thinking follows, the church engineered a smear campaign to portray her as a prostitute.

Langdon was right that "[e]veryone loves a conspiracy" (169). Brown, using discredited sources, tells a conspiracy tale like no other. Not only was Mary Magdalene Jesus' companion, but their relationship produced a child. And that bloodline lives today. Brown draws much of this conjecture from *Holy Blood, Holy Grail*. The authors of this 1982 nonfiction book go further in their depiction of Mary as the Grail:

> If our hypothesis is correct, the Holy Grail would
> have been at least two things simultaneously. On
> the one hand, it would have been Jesus' bloodline
> and descendants—the "Sang Raal," the "Real" or
> "Royal" blood of which the Templars, created by
> the Prieuré de Sion, were appointed guardians. At
> the same time the Holy Grail would have been,
> quite literally, the receptacle or vessel that received

and contained Jesus' blood. In other words it
would have been the womb of the Magdalen—and
by extension, the Magdalen herself.[1]

According to Brown's Leigh Teabing, "the marriage of
Jesus and Mary Magdalene is part of the historical record"
(245).

There is no credible historical record that Jesus was married. None. We will not even enter the debate as to whether Jesus was married or not. This is simply, from a biblical and historical perspective, a nonissue, despite even the patently false supposition that Jews in Jesus' time were somehow forbidden to remain unmarried (245).

Was Mary Magdalene a Prostitute?

There is no evidence that the early church tried to tarnish Mary Magdalene's reputation by making her out to be a prostitute. Any reference to her as a prostitute does not come from the Bible. Here is what we do know of Mary from the biblical record: Seven demons were cast out of her by Jesus (Luke 8:2); she witnessed the horror of the crucifixion (Matthew 27:32–56); she was present at the burial of Jesus (Matthew 27:57–61); she, along with two other women, went to anoint the body of Jesus (Mark 16:1); and she was the first person to see Jesus in his resurrected body (John 20:10–18).

Some have surmised that since her name and story appear immediately following the account of a prostitute, the two are one and the same woman (see Luke 7:36–8:2). But there is no biblical support for this conclusion. (Most historians agree that the reference to Mary Magdalene as a prostitute was started in the sixth century by Pope Gregory I.) Still others have conjectured that she is the anonymous woman caught in adultery. There is no evidence to support that assumption, either. Some have guessed that she might have been a prostitute simply because she came from

Magdala, which was often associated with prostitution. Once again, the Bible says no such thing. Any association of Mary of Magdala with either of the above-mentioned anonymous women would have been merely a result of conjecture—or very careless scholarship—probably dating to the Middle Ages, as opposed to a smear campaign.

We do know that Mary Magdalene was a follower of Christ. We also know that Jesus ministered to her, as he did to hundreds—perhaps thousands—of men and women. And—most important—we know that she was the first person ever to report that Jesus was risen from the dead. Instead of questioning her reputation, the Bible assigns to her one of the highest honors of all time: announcing the single most important event in history, the resurrection.

For that matter, the Bible does record that many so-called people of disrepute did believe and follow after Jesus. The apostle Matthew himself was called from the ranks of "sinners," being a traitorous tax collector, arguably lower in Jewish social standing than a prostitute (Matthew 9:9–13).

So even if Mary Magdalene could have been proved a prostitute, how could there have been any "smearing" on the part of biblical Christians? To the frustration of the religious leaders of the time, Jesus' way was to associate with and bring into his fold those who were considered outcasts.

HAS THE CHURCH HIDDEN THE HOLY GRAIL?

On the surface, *The Da Vinci Code* is about the search for the hiding place of the Holy Grail. At its core, there is a much greater message—a code we are attempting to crack. But let us look now to this quest for the Holy Grail. Is the church really suppressing knowledge of such an item through means that include extortion and murder?

The Grail lore came about in the latter part of the twelfth and early part of the thirteenth centuries. It varied from a simple dish a hermit saw in a vision to fantastic tales of miracles done by a cup or dish. The stories that tell of the quest for the Grail became intertwined with legends of King Arthur, but they all disappeared after the thirteenth century, later reappearing in the nineteenth century in a poem by Alfred Lord Tennyson (*Idylls of the King*) and music by Richard Wagner. And, of course, the latest manifestations have been in several twentieth-century films.

The Roman Catholic Church did not originate the idea of the Grail, nor does it promote the Grail as a sacred relic. From the *Catholic Encyclopedia*:

> Excepting Helanindus [a historian writing in the
> thirteenth century], clerical writers do not mention
> the Grail, and the Church ignored the legend com-
> pletely. After all, the legend contained the elements
> of which the Church could not approve. Its sources
> are in apocryphal, not in canonical, scripture, and
> the claims of sanctity made for the Grail were
> refuted by their very extravagance.[2]

Yet Langdon claims, "The Grail is literally the ancient symbol for womanhood, and the Holy Grail represents the sacred feminine and the goddess, which of course has now been lost, virtually eliminated by the Church" (238).

In Brown's code, the church is actively suppressing the identity of the Grail. This could not be further from the truth. The hard reality is, the Grail remains—as it has always been—an inconsequential legend to Christians of the real church: at best a novelty, but to most an aberration.

YES, WE BELIEVE THERE IS A HOLY GRAIL

Is there a real Holy Grail? No, there is no physical Grail. There is not a magic dish like the one mentioned in the medieval stories, nor is there the simple, wooden cup Indiana

Jones chooses in *Indiana Jones and the Last Crusade*. And we can say for certain that the Holy Grail is not, as Brown would have you believe, Mary Magdalene or her offspring.

But there is a spiritual sense in which the Holy Grail might be said to be real. The authors of *Holy Blood, Holy Grail* unknowingly hit on a truth in the legend of the Grail. They write that the Grail is "the receptacle or vessel that received and contained Jesus' blood." They are correct, but they are looking for this vessel in all the wrong places. In fact, this Grail can be seen clearly in Leonardo da Vinci's fresco, *The Last Supper*. Listen to Jesus' words during that meal:

> While they were eating, Jesus took a loaf of bread, and after blessing it he broke it, gave it to the disciples, and said, "Take, eat; this is my body." Then he took a cup, and after giving thanks he gave it to them, saying, "Drink from it, all of you; for this is my blood of the covenant, which is poured out for many for the forgiveness of sins" (Matthew 26:26–28 NRSV).

The Holy Grail is the receptacle of Jesus' blood, shed on the cross by a sinless Man to provide forgiveness for sinful men and women. But this Holy Grail is not a limited biological or ethnic reality (the physical seed of Jesus, as Brown contends); rather, it's a multiethnic, global, spiritual fellowship made up of all kinds of forgiven sinners. In other words, those who receive forgiveness through the blood of Jesus are the Holy Grail. The real church, made up of forgiven sinners from every gender, race, nation, and socioeconomic group, is the spiritual Holy Grail.

BROWN'S IDEAL CHURCH

What kind of church does Brown advocate? He tipped his hand in the book he wrote just prior to *The Da Vinci Code*.

Brown introduced Robert Langdon in *Angels and Demons*, another exciting, fast-paced novel with a religious theme underneath the action. In this book, Langdon is working side by side with Vittoria Vetra to prevent a disaster in the Vatican. During one of their conversations, the topic turns to faith. Vittoria tells Langdon:

> Faith is universal. Our specific methods for under-standing it are arbitrary. Some of us pray to Jesus, some of us go to Mecca, some of us study sub-atomic particles. In the end we are all just searching for truth, that which is greater than our-selves.[3]

Brown undermines the biblical picture of the church and substitutes his own vision in its place. Contrast Jesus' church (one in which sinners are saved through the blood sacrifice of God-become-man) with Brown's vision of the ideal church: one in which everyone is doing what feels good at the time; one in which there is acceptance of all beliefs without distinction.

CHAPTER 6
THE CANON: GNOSTIC VERSUS THE NEW TESTAMENT

*"Constantine commissioned and financed a new Bible,
which omitted those gospels that spoke of Christ's human traits and
embellished those gospels that made Him godlike…. The modern Bible
was compiled and edited by men who possessed a political agenda—
to promote the divinity of the man Jesus Christ and use his
influence to solidify their own power base"* (234).

The Bible is the best-selling book in the history of publishing. It has been translated into thousands of languages and is read by millions every day. Yet if what *The Da Vinci Code* says about the origins of this book are true ("The Bible is a product of man, my dear. Not of God" [231]), then the Bible is not the inspired Word that reveals the Creator to creation, but a cruel hoax that has deceived followers for thousands of years.

- Is it true that "more than eighty gospels were considered for the New Testament" but were turned down by the church and then destroyed (231)?
- Is it true that the Coptic Scrolls found near the village of Nag Hammadi, Egypt, in 1945, "highlight glaring discrepancies and fabrications … [of] the modern Bible" (234)?
- Is it true that these scrolls are "the earliest Christian records" (245)?
- Is it true that "many scholars claim that the early Church literally stole Jesus from His original followers, hijacking His human message, shrouding it in an

impenetrable cloak of divinity, and using it to expand their own power" (233)?

- Is it true that in the "secret gospels" genuine spiritual seekers can find the true Jesus (234)?

It is all true, if one can believe the reassuringly handsome and intelligent Robert Langdon, Harvard professor of religious symbology, who—with his courageous, bright, and beautiful cofugitive, Sophie Neveu—is on a search for truth wherever it may be found.

DON'T SHOOT THE CANON

First, a canon is not an enormous gun from antiquity found in museums. That is *cannon* with a double *n*. *Canon* with one *n* refers to the recognized list of authentic books that make up the Bible—both Old and New Testaments. *The Da Vinci Code* suggests that this list was created in the fourth century.

Canon in the Bible

Canon is a very biblical idea. Bible means "book," and the Christian faith is established in books and written documents. Here is the antithesis to Brown's version of the Bible's history—the first generations of the Christian movement stated loudly and clearly the biblical nature of their faith. They believed in a written Canon, beginning with the Old Testament; and they believed the Canon to be uniquely inspired by God himself.

Though Jesus did not write anything, he made sure there would be people, trained by him, who would bring his message to the world. To write his gospel, Luke indicates that firsthand eyewitnesses handed down their accounts directly to him (Luke 1:2); the apostle Peter claimed to be one of those "eyewitnesses" (2 Peter 1:16); the apostle John claimed to have "heard ... seen ... touched" Jesus (1 John

1:1); and Paul claimed to have been the last to see the risen Lord (1 Corinthians 15:8).

The apostle Peter, right from the outset of his first letter, flatly declared that Old Testament prophets foretold in their writings of Jesus' "sufferings" and "glories," and this fore-telling happened centuries before Jesus ever appeared in the flesh on earth. Even though the prophets of old probably didn't fully fathom what they were writing, they nevertheless faithfully communicated according to how they were inspired by the Holy Spirit, whom the apostle specified was sent by the "Spirit of Christ" (1 Peter 1:11–12).

It's important to understand that all biblical references to "prophets" and "prophesying" first and foremost mean God was speaking through those humans, less than that they were foretelling the future. In fact, many writings by prophets don't even foretell; rather, they forth-tell from God. In Peter's second letter, he reaffirmed that "prophecy never had its origin in the will of man, but men spoke from God as they were carried along by the Holy Spirit" (2 Peter 1:21).

Christ's Rock and the Apostles' Role

The Bible is full of eyewitness testimony, confirming God's written prophecy. This is the rock on which Christ promised to build his church (Matthew 16:18). Jesus said of the apostles who lived with him, watched him, heard him, and touched him: "He who listens to you listens to me" (Luke 10:16).

Paul used a different but parallel image to that of rock. He said that the apostles were the foundation of the church (Ephesians 2:20). There is no other foundation than this solid rock (1 Corinthians 3:11). The apostles and prophets formed the foundation by speaking and teaching but also by writing and exhorting coming generations to "guard what has been entrusted" (1 Timothy 6:20; see also 2 Timothy 1:12–14).

This witness of Paul—broadly accepted even by skeptics as written in the fifties of the first century—corroborates the word of Jesus to the apostle Peter and shows the flawed nature of Leigh Teabing's supposition: "The rock on which Jesus built His Church … was not Peter…. It was Mary Magdalene" (248). Again, we are dealing here with "fact-ion."

Here are a few more reasons to believe that a Canon was part of the church. From the beginning:

- "words of … prophecy" (Revelation 1:3) were read in public worship along with the Old Testament texts and thus had canonical authority in the churches (Colossians 4:16);
- Paul's writings were referred to as "Scriptures" by the apostle Peter (2 Peter 3:16);
- Paul referred to the gospel of Luke as "Scripture" (1 Timothy 5:18; see also Luke 10:7);
- Paul used the word *kanon* ("rule") when referring to the fundamental teaching of the apostles, which was to be followed and obeyed (Galatians 6:16).

The writings of the next generation of believers confirmed this understanding of the New Testament as Scripture. Ignatius of Antioch (AD 35–107), Polycarp (AD 69–115), the Epistle of Barnabas (AD 120), and Second Clement (AD 140), all referred to various New Testament books as "Scripture."

Two versions of Christianity did not develop simultaneously alongside each other, as *The Da Vinci Code* maintains. That would mean the church was born in total confusion with no clear, earth-changing message. Common sense demands that there was first orthodoxy, cemented by written, widely accepted texts produced by the first generation of believers. Then there was a deviant version followed by its own set of writings.

A written canon existed at the very beginning of the Christian faith. In fact, the early church already possessed the Canon of the Old Testament. And as they wrote the New Testament, they were consciously writing the conclusion to the Canon—the fulfillment of the Old Testament. The next generation received the New Testament this way.

Christianity and the Bible cannot be separated. If the Bible is truly the Word of God, as it claims to be, then Christians who claim to be followers of that God stake everything on it. It has been said, "The church did not create the Canon: the Canon created the church." In other words, it is the Word of God from the outside, given at key moments in history through his chosen messengers, that calls the people of God into existence. In the fourth century, the church merely published for the sake of clarity what it had always believed to be true.

An Unlikely Unanimity

As we have noted, on the first day of the church's history, the gospel was preached to representatives from almost every nationality—in their own languages (Acts 2:1–11). And the message spread. The church grew numerically and geographically at a phenomenal rate. Apostles scattered in all directions—Paul traveled to the Middle East and then to Europe; John went to Asia Minor; Matthew remained in Palestine; and Thomas perhaps went to India. The list goes on.

While the New Testament gives clear voice to the unity of the early church, as time passed and the church spread throughout the known world, it is understandable that not everyone had immediate access to all the books that constituted the Canon as it was at the beginning or as it was finally established. The early church was spread across vast distances, separated by months of travel, and often forced underground by persecution. It had no faxes, no telephones, no Internet, no TV, no radio. Had the early Canon not been well established very early in the church's history, it would never have survived as such an amazingly unified structure.

The Apocryphal Books

During this period there were three types of apocryphal books; that is, books whose origins were questioned: (1) the writings of apostolic and postapostolic fathers (late first and second centuries); (2) popular third-class literary entertainment (second and third centuries); and (3) heretical books, especially of a Gnostic nature (second to fourth centuries).

The Da Vinci Code calls the heretical books "secret gospels." This, though they were never considered canonical because the church recognized how far they were from the message of the canonical books.

None of the books in the three categories mentioned above fits in the canonical collection. As a religious scholar of a previous era, Kurt Aland affirmed, "It cannot be said of a single writing preserved to us from the early period of the Church outside the New Testament that it could be properly added to the canon."[1]

WERE EARLY ACCOUNTS BURNED?

The eccentric Teabing, supposing great expertise in the matter, states, "Constantine commissioned and financed a new Bible, which omitted those gospels that spoke of Christ's human traits and embellished those gospels that made Him godlike. The earlier gospels were outlawed, gathered up, and burned" (234).

There is no evidence that the text of the original Gospels was "embellished" in the fourth century. Scores and scores of copies of these Gospels already existed in the second century, establishing the text that was received in the fourth. There was no way the texts could have been altered. No one had the authority to call in from the very limits of the empire every last copy (which by the fourth century were numbering in the hundreds, perhaps thousands) to make the necessary alterations. This really is fiction.

The church established the Canon only in the sense of identifying publicly those books that from the earliest times had already imposed themselves on the faith of believers as intrinsically canonical. There were no canonical books written in the fourth century, nor were texts embellished in the fourth century. Again Kurt Aland, one of the editors of the most widely used Greek New Testament today, sizes up the situation: "[The Canon] was not imposed from the top, be it by bishops or synods, and then accepted by the communities.... The organized church did not create the canon; it recognized the canon that had been created."[2]

When Christians were no longer persecuted and the empire was at peace, the leaders of the far-flung church were finally able to meet together. When they did, they were not creating the Bible but merely clarifying and unifying once and for all what had been true from the beginning.

To determine what was canonical they asked a few simple questions:

1. Of the few books still in question, which ones agreed with the system of doctrine of the core books already unanimously accepted as canonical?
2. As historical witness to Jesus, which of the books in question were from the earliest church, from the pens of the apostles and their fellow workers?
3. Did these books have the same "ring of truth" and the mark of the inspiration of the Holy Spirit as the others? (It is a matter of faith that if God's Holy Spirit inspired his Word, he also protected it.)

There is a real danger today that, in the name of spiritual openness and inclusiveness, we can end up embracing the irrational and the contradictory—arguably, isn't this the real "blinding ignorance" we should be warned of from *The Da Vinci Code?*

The history of the Bible is clear and open. Orthodoxy has survived great difficulties, long separations, and intense persecution through courageous preaching, holy living, martyrdom, and the life-changing power of the gospel. *The Da Vinci Code*, and the majority scholarship that stands behind it, seeks to impose another version of history— a history of suspicion.

The Hollywood star Mel Gibson in speaking about his movie *The Passion of the Christ* gets it right: "Critics who have a problem with me don't really have a problem with me in this film. They have a problem with the four Gospels."[3] People's problem with the message of the Bible forces them to reinterpret or rewrite history.

In the new version of history presented by Brown, power-hungry bishops with political aims strategically take over the church and create a Bible in the image of their personal theological choices. But the story of the Canon will not allow such a twisting of history. The New Testament functioned with minor variations from the beginning as the Canon/Rock on which Jesus promised to build his church. That church has always believed in a gospel "once delivered unto the saints" (Jude 1:3 KJV) at a specific moment in history when God spoke definitively and uniquely through his Son (Hebrews 1:1–2).

This is the life-changing good news of God's act for lost sinners. Orthodoxy follows a straight line from the teaching of Jesus in the thirties to the writings of Paul and the other apostles in the latter half of the first century, to the final decrees of the ecumenical synods in the fifth century, seeking to preserve this original unique truth.

The Da Vinci Code uses a fictional structure to get its own message across. While seeming to advocate a courageous search for truth at any price, its real goal is to erode one of the fundamental characteristics of the Christian faith—the belief that the original message of the gospel, enshrined in the Bible, is the unique, inspired word from God himself, without which we are lost.

GNOSTIC GOSPELS

I (Peter) know a real-life equivalent to Robert Langdon. As I sat in that Harvard research seminar room, I caught sight of the brilliant Elaine Pagels. At the time, she was twenty-four and a rising star, one of the privileged handful of scholars to be included in a group studying those Nag Hammadi Gnostic texts that no one else had yet seen.

Pagels is now the Harrington Spear Paine Professor of Religion at Princeton University, and she has lived both a star-spangled life and a tragic life. She has become a world-class scholar, but she lost a husband to a mountaineering accident and a young child to illness. She writes freely about these losses and about her spiritual quest.

Pagels' book, *The Gnostic Gospels,* published when she was thirty-five, was an immediate best seller. Almost single-handedly, it moved the lost Nag Hammadi texts, perhaps the real heroes of *The Da Vinci Code*, from the ivory tower into the public square.[4] Writing with "the instincts of a novelist," as one reviewer said, she brought the Gnostic heretics to life and made them likeable. She presented Gnosticism (a religion of self-knowledge and of deep spiritual experience) as an alternate expression of early Christianity—the same story told from another side. To her, the Gnostic "Christians" are the forgotten victims and heroes of a class war waged by the politically powerful bishops.

A generation of scholars studied the fifty-two Coptic scrolls, only five of which are called "gospels," and produced an English translation in 1977.[5] Since that time, a handful of radical—some would say extremist—New Testament scholars associated with a group called the Jesus Seminar have sought to pull off a "palace revolution." In one generation, they have used these scrolls to redefine Jesus, rewrite the origins of the Christian faith, rewrite early church history, redefine the contents of the Canon, and completely reinterpret the Christian faith as a particular version of "Gnostic" spirituality.

Radical religious feminism has also found in these long-lost texts a gold mine of inspiration to recreate reality in the likeness of the "sacred feminine." The leader at the 1997 Gathering of Presbyterian Women ceremoniously laid the Bible aside and asked the 5,300 participants to consider new revelations—women's diaries and the "new" gospels, since the four gospels of the Bible were full of male, human bias.

The founder of the Jesus Seminar has vowed to take the "new scholarship" to the masses. With the publication of *The Da Vinci Code*, it has happened. Now many are asking if these "secret gospels" are the earliest, most authentic expression of original Christianity.

Is all this true? Have we been duped for centuries, and must we now be willing to give up faith in a shattered dream? Is the new version of Jesus where our true allegiance belongs?

How Early Are the Coptic Scrolls?

A few recognized scholars today claim that one of these "secret gospels," the Gospel of Thomas, is the second earliest Christian writing in existence, earlier than Matthew, Mark,

Luke, and John. Yet, the scholars who first began studying these documents didn't seem to make such claims. One expert on the Gospel of Thomas said in 1961, "[The Gospel of Thomas's] character is so far removed from the four canonical Gospels that it cannot be put on a par with them."[6]

So how do these recent scholars make their novel case? They use a strange argument based on a document mentioned in *The Da Vinci Code*, a scroll called "Q." Scholars looked at Matthew's gospel and Luke's gospel and noticed that long sections of the material were identical. So they examined only that shared material, setting aside the rest. They noticed that the shared material does not speak about the death and resurrection of Jesus. "Aha," they thought. "This means that both Matthew and Luke must have been using another scroll, from which they copied the material."

No one has ever found such a scroll. As far as anyone knows, it doesn't exist. But, having guessed it into existence, the scholars called it "Q" and argued that it had to be earlier than either Matthew or Luke. In fact, they said, "Q" has to be the earliest Christian writing. From these extracted verses made into a book, these scholars then made up a new picture of Jesus. They argued that the earliest followers of Jesus used this book as their only scripture and did not believe in the "later" picture of Jesus we get from the biblical Gospels. Because the Gospel of Thomas is similar in nature to the nonexistent book "Q" (not mentioning the death and resurrection, for example), it too must be one of the earliest books about Jesus and the true way to understand who he is.

The fact is, there is no need for "Q" to exist at all. There is a very simple explanation for the shared material in Matthew and Luke: As he wrote his gospel, Luke used material from Matthew's gospel as a faithful witness about certain things.

Which Really Came First?

Not one other scroll dug up along with the Gospel of Thomas has ever been dated so early. It apparently cannot be done; otherwise some scholar in the Gnostic camp would have tried it. The early case for a "Gnostic" Jesus stands or falls with the Gospel of Thomas. All the books of the New Testament can be plausibly dated prior to AD 70.[7]

The earliest likely date for the Nag Hammadi scrolls is around AD 150 and later, when Gnosticism as a system began to flourish. This date is accepted for the gospels of Philip and Mary. *The Da Vinci Code* draws its Holy Grail myth partly from these two gospels, claiming that they also predated the gospels that now appear in our New Testament.

The New Testament mentions that "false teachers" are coming, generally of a Gnostic kind.[8] Half-baked forms of Gnosticism were already emerging when the apostle Peter wrote of "cleverly devised myths" (2 Peter 1:16ff ESV) that would threaten Christian faithfulness to historic, divine revelation.

Two versions of Christianity did not develop alongside each other, as *The Da Vinci Code* maintains. The first message was the Christian message from Jesus and his apostles, established through widely accepted texts written by the first generation of believers. Later, there was a reactionary message, Gnostic heresy, which was cemented by its own set of writings.

The Christian chicken came before the Gnostic egg.

WHY IS GNOSTICISM SO ATTRACTIVE TODAY?

Brown's book is, as the French say, "the drop that makes the glass overflow" (or as English puts it, "the straw that breaks the camel's back"). With the appearance of *The Da Vinci Code*, related books such as those of Pagels on the ancient Gnostic texts are flying off bookstore shelves faster than they can be stocked—but for reasons much deeper than the success of a page-turner novel.

These Gnostic writings have reappeared at a time when patriarchy, doctrinal precision, canons, confessions, clearly defined sexual morality, church institutions, and authority are out. What's in? The personal spiritual quest, diversity, individualism, egalitarianism, and sexual liberation. And the prospect of finding ancient "Christian" scrolls that support this new era's spiritual viewpoint is, for many postmoderns, a dream come true.

The Best of Both Worlds?

Here we begin to decipher *The Da Vinci Code* and to suggest the real reason for its enormous popularity. The book appeals to many people because it expresses in such an engrossing way the new liberating religious option that has recently taken the West by storm.

The Da Vinci Code is a powerful form of religious propaganda. In an interview on ABC's *20/20* Dan Brown spoke about his "conversion" to a new way of thinking about the origins of Christianity. He also admitted that he saw himself as being on a mission to bring this religious message to mainstream America.

At a different level, scholar Elaine Pagels is on a similar mission. Pagels was once an evangelical Christian, but in an interview on National Public Radio she admitted to a fascination with the Gnostic texts, especially *Thunder, Perfect Mind*. Pagels is also interested in the blending of Christianity and Buddhism.[9] A number of the Jesus Seminar scholars, having also freed themselves from biblical orthodoxy, are on a similar religious mission.

The prophet Isaiah had to warn Israel of the temptation to blend biblical faith with other religions. Peter, Paul, and

John warned the early church of seductive myths in "Christian" apparel. The church must now warn Christians against new (but oh, so old) "clever" myths about the nature of the world.

All good myths are cleverly devised, to borrow the apostle Peter's term. Nothing is simple. We must keep all our wits about us in this debate about truth. The Bible warns us with great clarity that there is a huge distinction between these two forms of religious knowing:

- Revelation, which was inspired by the transcendent Lord, the Creator and Redeemer of the heavens and the earth, and
- Myths, which have a noninspired, human, or cultural source.

CHAPTER 7
THE CLASH OF THE SYMBOLS

A newly emerging power [took] over the existing symbols and
degrade[d] them over time in an attempt to erase their meaning.
In the battle between the pagan symbols and the
Christian symbols, the pagans lost (37).

Well folks, as you all know, I'm here tonight to talk to
you about the power of symbols" (9). As *The Da Vinci
Code* begins, this is how Robert Langdon opens his lecture at
the American University of Paris.

Well, folks, we are likewise here at whatever hour you
are reading our book, to write to you about the power of symbols. *The Da Vinci Code* employs powerful symbols to
communicate its mysterious code. In fact, it is no accident
that the very first chapter introduces a main character who is
lecturing on pagan symbolism.

The lead characters are experts in such symbolism.
Langdon is a Harvard professor of religious symbology and
author of a book, *Symbols of the Lost Sacred Feminine,* which
includes the iconography of goddess worship, fertility, Wicca,
and Isis. Allegedly, Leonardo da Vinci belonged to this arcane
school of thought (113) and was "an avid student of the
occult."[1] Jacques Saunière "knew more about pagan iconography than anyone else on earth" (77) and had "a passion for
relics relating to fertility, goddess cults, Wicca, and the sacred
feminine" (23).

At one level, the drama of the novel can be defined in the
conflict of symbols it evokes. "In the battle between the pagan
symbols and Christian symbols," says Langdon, "the pagans
lost" (37). What the pagans lost is now resurrected by no less

than Dan Brown himself. The battle is rejoined.

- Is it true that the symbolism of the circle is simply innocent (343)?
- Is it true that Baphomet is a harmless symbol for the goodness of sexuality and another way to speak of wisdom (316–321)?
- Is it true that Satan is the result of "the Church's attempts to recast the horned fertility god as a symbol of evil" to demonize its opponents (316)?
- Is it true that "the Church launched a smear campaign against the pagan gods and goddesses, recasting their divine symbols as evil" (37)?

THE POWER OF THE CIRCLE

There is nothing simpler than a circle, except, perhaps, a straight line, but the circle contains a universe of meaning. *The Da Vinci Code* honors the sun (339) and speaks of "[t]he simplicity of the circle" (343), which is used in ritual worship (316).

But, one may argue, there's nothing mysterious and powerful about a simple circle!

If the circle is so common, so innocent, so powerless, why are pagan groups the world over in love with "the power of the circle"? In ancient Egyptian religion, the circle stood for the all-inclusiveness of the sun, one of the powers of nature.[2] The early American non-Christian spiritualist Ralph Waldo Emerson even wrote a poem to "Circles," seeing himself and others as a unique planet with "no outside, no enclosing walls, no circumference to us."[3] From the center of such a limitless, circular universe the self reigns supreme.

The circle is not copyrighted by Emerson. It is also the most important symbol in the Wicca religion, a spiritual tradition that worships nature. In their basic ritual, Wiccans cast a "sacred circle" to capture the powers of the natural universe. "The circle is the sacred space created around an altar, either in a room or in a bush setting. It defines the area of ritual, holds within it the positive energy used for magick [sic], and wards off negative forces."[4]

"The power of the circle" is even taking on a political form. The Global Renaissance Alliance is a group of twenty-first-century, sophisticated, socially active people, many of whom are well-known promoters of the "New Spirituality." This group is determined to bring political change to America via a spirituality much like the one proposed in *The Da Vinci Code*. You can see on their Web site that they construct their program on "the ancient archetypal symbol of a circle, ... calling forth [the] ... magic[al] energies that represent unity, harmony and wholeness."[5]

Maybe you think we're going a little overboard here. How seriously should we take such a group? In case you have any doubts of the pagan and religious nature of this "political" vision, here is the statement from the Global Renaissance Alliance:

> The circle process embodies an ancient wisdom, the
> feminine wisdom of Sophia and Mary, Demeter,
> Cybele and Isis; the earthy and mystical wisdom of
> our tribal ancestors and our indigenous peoples.[6]

Politics is going spiritual in ways we never imagined! Did you ever believe a candidate for the presidency of the United States would say he was running for office "to enable the Goddess of peace to encircle within her arms all the children of this country and all the children of the world"?[7] Prepare yourself for goddess geopolitics!

THE "DIVINE, MAGICAL" PENTAGRAM

Good mystery novels get going with the first dead body. So does *The Da Vinci Code*. Jacques Saunière's corpse on the floor of the Louvre is not just any old dead body. It forms da Vinci's Vitruvian Man, the five points within a circle, which is the pentagram.

The pentagram, Langdon tells his Harvard class, "is one of the most powerful images you will see.... [It] is considered both divine and magical by many cultures" (96). It is one of the pre-Christian symbols favored by *The Da Vinci Code*, going back "four thousand years before Christ" (35), and is, says Langdon, "[p]rimarily a pagan.... religious symbol" (35).

Indeed, the pentagram was important to almost every ancient culture, including those of Latin America, India, China, and Egypt. Archaeologists have found the pentagram scratched on the walls of Neolithic caves and in Babylonian drawings where it marks the pattern of the planet Venus as it journeys through the skies.[8] The pentagram is another favored symbol of Wiccans[9] and holds much symbolic meaning in neopagan ritual.[10] It has also been used as a magical or occult symbol by the Pythagoreans, Masons, Gnostics, Kabalists, magicians, and satanists.[11]

Just as we associate Christianity with the cross and Judaism with the six-pointed star, pagans use the pentagram, a symbol of the magical rituals of pagan religions everywhere. It has never been used as a Christian symbol.[12]

It is surely significant that *The Da Vinci Code* dismisses the one obviously Christian symbol, the cross, as a symbol of violence and torture (145) and gives preference to a "peaceful cross ..." with four arms of equal length that "predated Christianity by fifteen hundred years" (145).

The circle that sometimes surrounds the pentagram represents "sacred space," typical of pagan religion. It is often used in pagan rituals as a focal point, as one Wiccan site proposes, to move "beyond the realms of physical form and our limited five senses, to explore the infinite possibilities that exist within the Universe."[13] This is one example of the spirituality described in the previous chapter.

The pentagram is sometimes seen with a goat's or ram's head within it, called Baphomet. Who is Baphomet?

Baphomet

In *The Da Vinci Code* Baphomet is a harmless "pagan god" (316), symbol of sexuality and an anagram for wisdom, or Sophia (318–321). He is not a symbol for Satan, since most pagans do not believe Satan exists.

Baphomet, as the horned fertility god, is certainly pre-Christian. The most familiar image of Baphomet portrays him seated, as a winged, goat-headed and goat-footed man with a woman's breasts, a flame on his forehead, and a phallus at his groin.[14]

In the twentieth century, German occultists formed the secret Ordo Templi Orientis (Order of Templars in the East). As head of their British section, they installed the English occultist Aleister Crowley, who took Baphomet as his magical name. In the 1960s, Simon LaVey established the goat-headed Baphomet within a circle as the sign of the present Church of Satan.[15]

Whether used in the nature-worshipping Wiccan kind of spirituality or in the personalized satanist kind, Baphomet is a symbol of paganism, which has nothing to do with the Bible. With regard to Satan in the main, Wiccans will not admit satanists into their celebrations because they claim Satan is a creation of Christianity.[16] We find the same approach in *The Da Vinci Code*.

Satan

Like some contemporary religious liberals, Brown finds no place in true spirituality for personal evil or a personal devil. He dismisses "[t]he modern belief in a horned devil known as Satan," as "the Church's attempts to recast the horned fertility god as a symbol of evil" (316).

Elaine Pagels, famous for her book on the Gnostic Gospels, wrote another book, *The Origin of Satan*,[17] which lends academic support to the Wiccan belief about Satan. Pagels argues that Satan, or the Devil as an evil being, emerged to prominence only out of the New Testament and was used to affirm one group's beliefs while demonizing the group's opponents.

Pagels places herself in a superior tradition in which she includes the Gnostics, Francis of Assisi, and Martin Luther King. She dismisses the words of Jesus, who said to those who opposed him, "You belong to your father, the devil" (John 8:44), and the words of Paul, who called those who preached another gospel "servants" of Satan (2 Corinthians 11:15).

The Da Vinci Code refuses to admit the existence of Satan, and in the same way says that the term *heretic* was created by the church in Constantine's time to demonize those who held to the religion contained in the Gnostic texts (234). *The Da Vinci Code* takes the same line as Pagels, who popularized the same Gnostic texts.

What if Pagels and *The Da Vinci Code* are wrong, duped by the "father of lies," who, as C. S. Lewis notes in *The Screwtape Letters*, loves humans to deny Satan's existence? We firmly believe what the New Testament teaches: There is real evil in the universe, and it has a personal source. By making this statement, we are not demonizing people, but warning them that real demons can deceive and influence them. We didn't write the Bible. It is the Bible that reminds us that all human beings are made in the image of God, and we cannot escape the cosmic struggle between right and wrong. Evil is a mystery, but it is not another face of God, the good Creator.

As Paul says, there is nothing in common between Christ and Satan (2 Corinthians 6:15). Good and evil cannot mix. Good and evil cannot be rolled into one happy, inclusive circle. In fact, Christians believe that evil is the exclusion—the separation from good—from God.

THE GODDESS

The inclusive circle is most clearly expressed in the symbol of the Goddess or the "sacred feminine" (238). The proof? The secret society, whose mission is to preserve the "real" truth of Christianity, is not Christian at all. As the book says, the Priory of Sion is "the pagan goddess worship cult" (113). The Priory's goal is to undo the evil perpetrated by "Constantine and his male successors" in the church, who "demonized the sacred feminine, obliterating the goddess from modern religion forever" (124).

Goddess in the Past

While claiming to be calmly objective and inclusive, *The Da Vinci Code* accuses the church of "launch[ing] a smear campaign against the pagan gods and goddesses, recasting their divine symbols as evil" (37). Nobody seems to have a corner on "smearing," for *The Da Vinci Code*'s attack on the church simply fails to discuss the theological reasons for Christianity's refusal of paganism. At the same time, the novel betrays its own deeply religious commitments to a "pre-Christian" (36) pagan spirituality (specifically, "the pentacle's true origins"), which it finds "actually quite godly" and its symbols "divine" (37).

The Goddess certainly is pre-Christian. She emerges from the mists of time, out of the East, as the savior from death. She manifested in many forms throughout the ancient ages, but the ancient Goddess is on a roll again these days.

Goddess in the Present

You may think American religion is in crisis. Not so, according to some. It is only in transformation. *When God Becomes Goddess*, a recent book of "Christian" theology, argues that "certain elements of traditional religious belief and practice [i.e., Christianity] are passing away and a new kind of religiosity is poised to take its place."[18] The religiosity that is ready to take its place is that of the Goddess.

The Goddess has also entered the popular mainstream through witchcraft. Hollywood and television have recently produced a series of movies and programs that takes us into bewitched territory. Hot Topic, an in-your-face clothes store for teenagers in our local mall, includes a rack of books on popular witchcraft. *Jennifer Hunter's 21st Century Wicca: A Young Witch's Guide to the Magical Life* is a best seller. Officially sanctioned Wiccan services now take place on army bases and in prisons throughout the land, and witch clergy perform marriages with the formal blessing of the New York City Council.

Jean Houston was a friend and counselor of First Lady Hillary Clinton during the 1990s. Houston believes our society needs to be rebuilt through the myth of the goddess Isis and her consort Osiris.[19] Our leaders are promoting the goddess of magic and the underworld as the savior who can bring us social, cultural, and spiritual transformation. They reason that the Gnostic "Christians" worshipped the mysteries of Isis, the Great Mother,[20] so as their texts are reread and trusted, their gods are revived. The title of a book written a few years ago expresses *The Da Vinci Code*'s deep message: *The Once and Future Goddess: A Symbol for Our Time.*[21] The old Goddess has come over the seas of time and landed on our shores with plans to transform us!

The "sacred feminine" really means the reign of Mother Nature. Nature and its forces determine everything. The sacred feminine assures us that everything in nature, including our inner self, is divine.

Joseph Campbell, who was a guru to George Lucas, director of *Star Wars*, said, "In religions where the god or creator is the mother, the world is her body. There is nowhere else."[22] Campbell was not an atheist, as you can see. He was plenty spiritual. But his spirituality was pagan. "God" is a word he used to mean the divinity of all natural things. He didn't use the word to mean a God who is outside creation and who is in fact its origin. Campbell's god was a kind of impersonal presence, to be found everywhere, in everything.[23]

THE GODDESS COMES TO AMERICA

The symbol of the Goddess and the spirituality it produces find no place in biblical faith. Nevertheless, the publishing arm of a mainline Christian denomination commends to the faithful the work of a theologian/pagan priestess, and says of her book, *Celebrating Her*,

> Deep within the womb of the earth lies a memory of
> a sacredness nearly buried under the weight of patri-
> archy.... More and more women—especially those
> with Christian backgrounds—are being drawn to
> this empowering, goddess-centered worship.[24]

Readers of our book are warned that the Goddess will not lead them into Christian worship, as Sue Monk Kidd's book joyfully asserts, but right out of it. Her title says it all: *The Dance of the Dissident Daughter: A Woman's Journey from Christian Tradition to the Sacred Feminine*.[25] This is at the core of what the sacred feminine means!

In our own backyard, San Diego, there is a project to welcome all those who make the exit. A group of Goddess worshippers plans to build a temple to the Goddess called the Center of the Divine Feminine. Amenities will include a five-hundred-person worship hall, a large flat area for circle ceremonies, fountains, statuary, a maypole, a peace pole, prayer flags, a fire pit, labyrinths, hot baths, natural water ponds, and herb and vegetable gardens.[26] The Temple of Diana/Artemis (a form of Isis), one of the wonders of the ancient world that dominated the city of Ephesus at the time of Paul, immediately jumps to mind. This is no longer fiction. For, as this pagan movement gains financial clout and institutional visibility, we are surely seeing only the beginning of the power of the sacred feminine.

An ex–Roman Catholic theologian with two doctorates, Mary Daly, who now calls herself an eco-feminist lesbian witch, welcomes this journey out from Christianity as "the Second Coming of the Goddess." She declares, in sobering terms,

> The antichrist and the Second Coming are synonymous. This Second Coming is not the return of Christ but a new arrival of female presence.... The Second Coming, then, means that the prophetic dimension in the symbol of the great Goddess ... is the key to salvation from servitude.[27]

Symbols are very important to us. We look to symbols as a type of road map to lead us along the way, and the symbols we choose to heed can determine our quality of life here—and in the hereafter.

So again, we are faced with a choice, in this case between symbols—the cross of Christ or the symbols of paganism (Wicca, witchcraft, the sacred feminine, Baphomet, and the Goddess). The question before us is, which version of history and faith with all of its accompanying symbols is true, and which is a lie?

But that question itself has a Christian bias, doesn't it? Because from a pagan view of the world, the truth and the lie would also simply be encircled as one and the same—like life and death, good and evil, truth and lie become one. Echoing the words of Pilate as he sent Jesus to the cross, the pagan has to ask, "What is truth?" (John 18:38). And in the same breath, is there such a thing as a lie?

But we all know there is such thing as a lie, don't we? We know bigotry is a lie; we know that dehumanizing women as sex objects is a lie. And what of the Gnostic and pagan claim that the biblical Gospels are lies? If we're willing to call something false, there must also be a choice of truth.

The Jesus of the Christian New Testament isn't in the least confused on the matter. He unabashedly calls himself the sole source of truth—in fact, he literally declares that he himself is "the truth" (as well as the "life," and the only "way" to God, as recorded by that firsthand witness, John [14:6]). But to the pagan way of thinking and believing, should it really matter to us if Jesus was lying—if truth and lies are all in the circle of oneness? It's a question that should give all thinking seekers great cause for concern, especially if the premise of their pursuit is that it doesn't matter if they are following a lie. After all, what's the difference between truth and lie?

Now with the question of "is there such a thing as truth" before us, let's consider the question of why we should care about all of this symbolism. To the authentic Christian's way of thinking, symbolism has an ironic potential for being a profound distraction from truth. (Admittedly, that's because we believe there is such a thing as an absolute, knowable truth.) And just as idolatry amounts to worshipping the created instead of the Creator (the tree, rather than the Maker of the tree), so symbols can become our obsessive focus of devotion. In fact, the symbol can block our view of the truth to which it is supposed to be pointing.

Christians do not claim to worship the cross, but rather they worship God the Son who hung on the cross. They do not claim to worship an empty tomb, but rather the Christ who rose from the tomb. Symbols can be a great help for our understanding. But what (or better, who) is it that we are trying to understand?

It all comes full circle (as it were) back to the central question: Is the Jesus of the Christian Gospels who he says he is? Is he really God, or is he simply a distraction? Is the Jesus of the Bible the truth—or a lie?

CHAPTER 8
CRACKING THE CODE

"You gonna have to serve somebody. It may be the devil or it may be the Lord." Bob Dylan, "Gotta Serve Somebody" [1]

The stone towers and green copper roof of the Church of Saint-Sulpice stand out against the dull gray of the Parisian skyline. In this church, *The Da Vinci Code* sets the brutal murder of Sister Sandrine by Silas, an albino monk. In passing, the story mentions that the church was built over the ruins of a temple to Isis (88) and contains a colossal pyramid-shaped obelisk, which, in Egyptian religion, symbolized the rays of the sun (104). In this seemingly minor detail, we begin to see the "code."

The drama of the novel occurs on two levels.

At the level of the plot, heroes track down the Holy Grail, outsmarting adversaries and overcoming resistance from all directions.

At the level of the code, a deep subplot—the "sacred feminine"—heroically emerges from the shadows of the past. Against all odds, this philosophical heroine will undo the male power of the institutional church and banish to the cultural margins "third-century [Christianity, its views on women, and its] laws" that are "not workable in today's society" (416).

THE "NEW AGE" OF AQUARIUS

The Saint-Sulpice church, an impressive icon of Christianity, proudly occupies the modern public square. But the novel uncovers the irony of the church's real foundations: Goddess-worshipping paganism. Those foundations, suppressed for centuries, are rising again to displace the pretender and to reclaim their rightful place. The old, earlier, and authentic spirituality is replacing the later imposter. Pre-Christian, peace-loving "matriarchal paganism" and the "sacred feminine" will overcome violent "patriarchal Christianity" and the faith of our power-hungry macho church fathers (124). In short, the pre-Christian Goddess will replace the God of the Bible.

For many in our culture, the new "gospel" announced by *The Da Vinci Code* is good news. The Age of Aquarius replaces the Age of Pisces (401). "The Vatican faces a crisis of faith unprecedented in its two-millennia history," which also marks the end of "the two-thousand-year-long astrological Age of Pisces—the fish, which is also the sign of Jesus" (267). The Priory of Sion has been "waiting for the right moment in history to share their secret. A time when the world is ready to handle the truth" (295), [a time when] "we are entering the Age of Aquarius—the water bearer—whose ideals claim that man will learn the truth and be able to think for himself" (268).

Since the 1960s, modern mystics have hailed this "New Age" of Aquarius as the return of pagan spirituality. They call the Age of Pisces the "Christian interlude"—a parenthesis between two eras of paganism. Since the sixties, American history has witnessed a revolution far more powerful than the one that established this country as an independent nation. The recent revolutionaries have cut us free from our Christian-inspired past. In one generation, they have established new and radical views of the family, education, morals, marriage, sexuality, spirituality, and God. Their views have become the new politically correct orthodoxy.

At the risk of our sounding as if we're ringing the alarms of vast conspiracies, it's hard not to see a connection between the supposedly passé movement of the sixties generation and the neopaganism of today. The times have changed, and the new influencers, including Dan Brown, are rewriting history. Furthermore, it's simply naïve to dismiss the significant influence that this worldview is having on the media, education, and politics. Beliefs do impact how we live and the choices we make.

For nearly a generation, radical feminists have recommended "a new view of reality." In some churches, preachers speak of a Jesus whose body rotted in the grave. This new thinking will bring about "a new science and spirituality," a "new politics and economics, where the old nation state ... will wither away." All this will come about, in particular "through the reaffirmation and celebration of the transformative mysteries symbolized by the Chalice."[2]

According to *The Da Vinci Code*, this age "has arrived" as "the End of Days" (268). Marie, Jacques Saunière's "wife," declares with the conviction of a believer, "We are beginning to sense the need to restore the sacred feminine," and exhorts Langdon with the passion of a missionary: "Sing her song. The world needs modern troubadours" (444).

Toward Global Religious Unity

Another church building makes the point clearer. Langdon hears the call to action as he gazes up at Rosslyn Chapel, a church supposedly built by the Templars who, according to one of the novel's well-crafted sayings, "had left no stone uncarved" (434). In this chapel, known as "the Cathedral of Codes," everything comes together (432). In this chapel the Isis foundations, so hidden at the Saint-Sulpice church, are exposed in all their glory. The carvings are the code.

> Each block [of the chapel] was carved with a symbol ... to form a bizarre multifaceted surface
> (436).... Christian cruciforms, Jewish stars, Masonic seals, Templar crosses, cornucopias, pyramids,

astrological signs, plants, vegetables, pentacles, and roses … Rosslyn Chapel was a shrine to all faiths … to all traditions … and, above all, to nature and the goddess (434).

The code stands for the unity of all faiths, founded on the worship of nature and the Goddess. This global faith will include a new pope and a church that follows him into pagan unity—the blending of opposing religions and philosophies into one, or syncretism (415–416).

Such an idea is far from novel. A second-century AD visitor to Apollo's temple at Didyma (in present-day Turkey) described it as a "circle of altars to every god."[3] One pagan priest of the period described himself as a "priest of all the gods."[4]

The vision of global religious unity drives many spiritual people in our time. As one modern Isis priestess put it, "It may be that Sophia/Isis is about to be … a beacon to Christians, Jews, Gnostics and Pagans alike."[5] Isis will bring religious unity on her pagan terms, this time on a planetary scale. If such a synthesis can be pulled off in America, says a United Methodist lesbian professor at Harvard, it would be "the greatest form of lasting leadership we [could] offer the world."[6] America's new religious calling is to develop a unified spirituality that will save the planet. For this new calling, we will also need a new Jesus.

Recalling an earlier quote in *American Jesus: How the Son of God Became a National Icon*,[7] the author argues that "Jesus won't become a national figure unless he can move outside Christianity." A non-Christian Jesus? Such was the Jesus of the Gnostic texts, and such is the Jesus of *The Da Vinci Code*.

In our fractured world of autonomous, unconnected people, the Goddess brings good news. It is claimed she will put our world together again. She will unite ecological wisdom, economic justice, human rights, women's liberation, equality and harmony between the sexes, pan-sexual freedom, personal significance, global peace, religious unity, utopian dreams, life on our own terms, and deep spirituality.

AN IDEOLOGICAL CALL TO ARMS

This ideology is what the *The Da Vinci Code* believes and teaches in story form. The book is written from a particular religious ideology. It is not a neutral fictional tale that adds a few historical facts for a ring of truth. It is a propaganda piece for a religious worldview. And that's fair enough, because it could be said that authors' worldviews impact any work of fiction. But readers of Brown's novel need to realize that his commitment to neopagan religious assumptions also colors his choice of "facts" and everything he affirms through his characters.

It is at this deep spiritual level that the book's attack on Christianity is the most vicious. We must, of course, answer its digs at the Bible and the authentic Jesus. However, the real significance of the book is its clear intention to undermine the very foundation of biblical faith and to establish in its place an opposing religious system. Because Brown has adopted the pagan worldview, he is not content to shoot a few BBs at the facts of church history. He wants to blow a hole in the foundations of the worldview of the Bible.

Under the guise of a novel, *The Da Vinci Code* is an ideological call to arms. During wartime, codes are useful for communicating crucial messages in hidden ways. As much as we wish we could ignore it, there is a spiritual war for the human soul. Two views of religion are warring in our day, and simply pretending otherwise won't make it go away. There might be hundreds of factions (religions) with their unique little agendas, but ultimately they all will eventually align themselves under two fundamental alliances: pagan monism and biblical theism.

Pagan Monism …

The religious worldview of *The Da Vinci Code* celebrates the soft, inclusive womb of the Goddess, from which everything emerges and to which it all returns. In this vision, the universe is one, so it can be called monism (think "one-ism"). Remember the circle in the previous chapter? According to monism, everything is in the circle—the divine, the human, animals, rocks, trees. Everything, according to this worldview, shares the same nature. There is no other circle, no other reality. In the divine union of nature and humanity, everything is possible. When we understand this "all is one" mentality, we can better understand *The Da Vinci Code*'s Hieros Gamos or "sacred marriage." The book's heroes come to grips with this shocking group-sex rite because it represents an ultimate spiritual experience—one shared, it is claimed, by all religions. It is known under several names: the unio mystica—the "mystical union," "deification" (becoming divine), "the seventh, highest mansion," "holy marriage," or "unitive vision."[8]

But with all of her diverse representations and forms, it is important to understand that the Goddess is only a symbol. She personifies the divine mystery in all things. Her ladyship exists only to express the fact that there is no personal deity. The "divine feminine" is an impersonal "force" that animates everything.

… versus Biblical Theism

There is one worldview that cannot fit into the soft circle of the pagans: theism, the time-tested worldview of the Bible. It cannot fit into the pagan, monistic circle because it honors God as Lord and Creator—as being outside the circle—the transcendent God, the God who is beyond his created order. The Christian God is above his creation. God and the universe are distinct, as distinct as a painter from his painting, as distinct as da Vinci from his *Last Supper*.

C. S. Lewis wrote, "God is a particular Thing."[9] God is not some kind of energy contained in the monistic circle, or "the circle of life." He is outside it. In contrast to the increasingly popular notion of the circle of life, the Bible reveals a very different view of God. The prophet Isaiah, in the eighth century BC, said of Yahweh, "He sits enthroned above the circle of the earth" (Isaiah 40:22). God has his own place, his own domain of existence. No created circle of life can contain him.

That is what we mean when we say that God is holy. "Holy" means "set apart" for a special place or function. God has a special place as Creator distinct from our place as creatures. We honor this understanding of God when we pray to "Our Father in heaven" (Matthew 6:9). That Father is the source of our personhood and the designer of our intricate universe. C. S. Lewis also wrote that the pagan god who is everything (and thus, in a sense, nothing) appears as a "mere zero," a "nonentity," a "featureless generality."[10]

Behind the debates and conflicting facts, at its core *The Da Vinci Code* is a radical redefinition of God as the impersonal force of nature.

NOTHING HAS CHANGED

The Da Vinci Code is a reader-friendly, airbrushed version of a spirituality that denies the essence of biblical faith and, in particular, the biblical revelation of God. This spirituality is not a version of Christianity, as contemporary skeptics claim by appealing to the early Gnostics. It is instead a denial of all that Christianity holds dear.

In a sense, nothing has changed. In the ancient world, there were two kinds of Gnostics: those with no relationship to Christianity, and those who tried to pass themselves off as Christians. In the early centuries of the church, Christian leaders went through the same process we have presented in this book. They consistently showed that Gnosticism was a religion different from true Christianity.

Tertullian, a Christian historian of those early days, spoke of the Gnostics' "blasphemy against the Creator,"[11] saying "they make no distinction between pagans and believers in their churches."[12] He charged that "they have commerce with magicians, [peddlers], astrologers and philosophers."[13]

Paganism, whether ancient or modern, stands in opposition to the Christian message of the Bible. The new manifestation of paganism is forcing Christians to go through the same process of examining their faith as the early Christians did when the secret scrolls of the ancient Gnostics were first written.

Old Battle, New Culture

In the first three centuries of the church, Christians fought on two fronts. On the outside, they were persecuted by the pagan authorities of imperial Rome who forced them to confess "Caesar is Lord." On the inside, they had to withstand the Gnostic wolf in sheep's clothing who claimed to be Christian but adopted the pagan spirituality of the Roman Empire. We are now seeing a repeat of this two-front battle.

As our culture becomes a more decadent Rome,[14] our struggle for truth resembles that of the early church as we, too, face those who call themselves believers in Christ but are really Gnostics. After two thousand years, the conflict over spiritual truth remains.

The Da Vinci Code implies that the conflict is between objective historians and honest truth-seekers on one hand, and a closed-minded, intrusive church on the other. The fact is, we all find ourselves in a struggle for ultimate truth, fought with religious zeal on both sides.

Gods and Goddesses, or God?

The Da Vinci Code's spirituality shows up early in human history. The opening declaration of the Bible—"In the beginning God created the heavens and the earth" (Genesis 1:1)—is announced into a social context of Egyptian paganism; in particular, that of the worship of Isis, goddess of magic and the underworld. That same truth of God the transcendent Creator is repeated as Israel enters Canaan where Baal and Asherah, the god and goddess of fertility, were worshipped as the forces of divine nature.

In the ninth century BC, Elijah called Israel to forsake these gods in order to serve the true and living God (1 Kings 17–19). In the eighth century BC, the prophet Isaiah constantly contrasted the God of creation and redemption with the gods of Babylonian paganism (Isaiah 40–49). But the people were stubborn. Through the Bible comes a constant refrain that Israel had joined herself to Baal with disastrous consequences.

This is a history of conflict between two different religions vying for people's souls. Biblical religion and paganism are mutually exclusive. The Bible's claim to uniqueness is not motivated by narrow-mindedness, intolerance, or fear. It is unique in its radically different definition of God.

When we get to the New Testament, we see that Jesus, the founder of Christianity, built on the Old Testament. He warned about praying like the pagans (Matthew 6:7) and spoke of only two ways: the kingdom of God or the kingdom of Satan (Matthew 12:25–28). He reminded his audience that no one could know the Father without coming through him, the Son.

THE CHOICE

After his conversion to Christianity, Bob Dylan sang the song, "You gonna have to serve somebody, … it may be the devil or it may be the Lord." *The Da Vinci Code* and the book you are now reading show the choice everyone has to make. It is the same choice Elijah put before God's people: "How long will you waver between two opinions? If the LORD is God, follow him" (1 Kings 18:21).

There are only two religious paths, only two ways we can relate to the divine. Is God just nature or is he the Creator of nature? Your answer to that question changes everything you think and do. You are religious whether you realize it or not. Everyone worships and serves something. Either you will worship and serve "the creation," or you will worship and serve "the Creator—who is forever praised" (Romans 1:25).

WHICH GOOD NEWS?

Paganism and Christianity both offer good news. Both propose redemption. Paganism proposes liberation from the Creator to do one's own thing and to figure out how to save oneself. The Bible proposes reconciliation with the Creator, who comes to his creation as Savior. No one who truly seeks that Savior will be turned away.

The circle representing all of creation and God who is above and beyond his creation are separate in two ways. First, we human creatures and God (the divine Creator) are different by nature. For instance, God has no beginning. We do. God knows everything. We don't. And there are many other differences.

Second, we are separated by something else. In our most honest moments, moments when we are alone, every one of us knows that something within us is broken. It needs to be fixed. We even have a sense that we do not measure up. It might even be described as a sense of moral inferiority. Sometimes it is called guilt. We don't like to admit this to anyone, but it is true of all of us. The reason we feel as though something is broken is because something *is* broken. The reason we feel guilty is because we *are* guilty.

The God Who Came to Us

All of us were made for the purpose of enjoying a wonderful relationship with the Creator God himself. But something devastated that relationship. It is called sin. As a result, a gap exists between us, as the created, and God the Creator. Every honest human feels this sense of estrangement, of loss, but it is not merely something felt. It is very real. And it's that state of separation—the "great divorce," as C. S. Lewis calls it—that is the essence of sin, much more so than the actions we've done. The "sins" that we commit and for which we feel more or less guilty are the symptoms of the real problem—being separated from God. That was the original sin of Eden, where the gap was introduced—where we first became our own gods (Genesis 3:4).

Furthermore, we can't close the gap. We can't fix the brokenness. We can't get to him. So he must come to us. Only God can fix it. And God did fix it. He actually brought himself and the circle (us) together. He connected them. How? God decided to become "downwardly socially mobile" and take on human flesh. To become like us. And that is what he did, when God came in human form, in Jesus.

But there's more.

For a perfect and holy God to be bridged to something broken and sinful, the sinful one needs to be changed. So Jesus, who never sinned, took upon himself the responsibility for our sin. We were then declared, in the legal jurisprudence of the universe, to be free of our sins. Not guilty! Romans 8:1 insists, "There is now no condemnation for those who are in Christ Jesus."

Those who will accept the gift are simply no longer responsible for their sin—their gap. What really makes us no longer responsible for our broken and sinful condition? What activates this reality? It is activated when we acknowledge the truth of it—that there is a gap of sin, and we want nothing more of it. We repent of it—we cross over and leave it behind.

Then the arc and the circle come together. We feel the passionate and loving arms of God wrapped around us. Then the sense of estrangement and loss leave. Jesus said, "I have come that they may have life, and have it to the full" (John 10:10). That's what happens when we are connected back to God!

This incredible truth about Jesus makes sense of Teabing's remark that "Jesus Christ was a historical figure of staggering influence, perhaps the most enigmatic and inspirational leader the world has ever seen" (231). A sex ritual with Mary Magdalene that produces a child hardly explains the influence of Jesus. Only a redeeming act of God with cosmic proportions can explain the impact of Jesus on the world. Only the biblical witness finally makes sense of Teabing's admission: Jesus is the Savior of the world (John 4:42).

Intimate Communion, True Joy

Our book does not intend to whitewash the obvious faults and misdeeds of those in the past who misrepresented Christ's church on earth. (Indeed, we join with any authentic Christian today in acknowledging our own faults and failures—the gap has been bridged, but God's changing our circles is the work of a lifetime—literally, our lifetime on earth.) Our book is also not an attempt to recover some lost "golden age" of the past. Its purpose has been, through a critical response to a major popular literary achievement, to clarify the two timeless religious options before which every human being must stand.

It is our firm belief and personal experience that there is comfort in the fact of an outside God to whom we can turn, who has promised not to turn us away if we seek him. There is a real Redeemer who offers real forgiveness and deals definitively with our nagging guilt. We can relax in the control God has over the world. We have the possibility of truly forgiving others. We can have intimate communion with him and joy in serving him. We can find our place in the world!

As the authors of this book, it is our hope and prayer that God, the unique Creator and Savior, will use these pages to draw those wandering Teabings of the world who have recognized the greatness of Jesus, that they may find the true Holy Grail of the gospel: Jesus himself, the true Savior of the world.

NOTES

Chapter 1

1. Dan Brown, *The Da Vinci Code* (New York: Doubleday, 2003), 235.

2. David Klinghoffer, "Books, Arts and Manners," *National Review* (8 December 2003).

3. Dan Brown, interview by Matt Lauer, *The Today Show*, NBC, 9 June 2003.

4. *Bookpage* (April 2003).

5. Juli Cragg Hilliard, "ABC Special Examines *Da Vinci Code* Ideas," *Publishers Weekly*, Religion Bookline.

Chapter 2

1. George Trevelyan, *A Vision of the Aquarian Age* (Walpole, NH: Stillpoint Publishing, 1984), 161, cited in Ray Yungen, *A Time of Departing: How a Universal Spirituality Is Changing the Face of Christianity* (Silverton, OR: Light House Trails, 2002), 24.

2. William Johnson, *Letters to Contemplatives* (New York: Orbis Books, 1991), cited in Yungen, ibid., 29.

3. See Stanislav Grof, *Future of Psychology: Lessons from Modern Consciousness Research* (New York: State University of New York Press, 2000), 5.

4. Stephen Prothero, *American Jesus: How the Son of God Became a National Icon* (New York: Farrar, Straus and Giroux, 2004), reviewed by Justin Pope, Associated Press (12 February 2004).

5. "From the New Physics to Hinduism," karma2grace.org, http://www.karma2grace.org/articles.htm.

6. Barry Long, *Meditation: A Foundation Course* (Mullumbimby, Australia: Barry Long Books, 1996), 13.

7. *Tripartite Tractate* 124.21ff.

8. *Apocryphon of James* 4:19–21. Walter Burkert, *Ancient Mystery Cults* (Cambridge, Mass.: Harvard University Press, 1987), 69, notes the same tendency in pagan mystery religions.

9. See the apology for this claim in Virginia Ramey Mollenkott, *Omnigender: A Trans-Religious Approach* (Cleveland, Ohio: The Pilgrim Press, 2001), 41, 74.

10. *Gospel of Truth* 25:1–7.

11. Shirley MacLaine, *Going Within: A Guide for Inner Transformation* (New York: Bantam Books, 1989), 197.

12. C. S. Lewis, *The Four Loves* (New York: Harcourt, 1960).

Chapter 3

1. Steven Goldberg, *Why Men Rule: A Theory of Male Dominance* (Chicago: Open Court, 1993), 14, 18, 35.

2. Alvin J. Schmidt, *Under the Influence* (Grand Rapids, Mich.: Zondervan, 2001), 98.

3. Verena Zinserling, *Women in Greece and Rome* (New York: Abner Schram, 1972), 39.

4. Jenny Gibbons, "Recent Developments in the Study of the Great European Witch Hunt, Covenant of the Goddess," http://www.cog.org/witch_hunt.html.

5. Ibid.

6. Robin Briggs, *Witches and Neighbors* (New York: Penguin, 1998).

7. Ross Clifford and Philip Johnson, *Jesus and the Gods of the New Age* (Colorado Springs:Victor Books , 2003).

8. http://www.cog.org/witch_hunt.html.

9. Robin Morgan, *Women's Voices: Quotations by Women,* Jone Johnson Lewis, http://www.womenshistory. about.com/library/qu/blqumorg.htm.

Chapter 4

1. So well established are Paul's dates that few modern scholars, in their work on Paul, even bother to mention the subject.

2. Hans Conzelmann, *1 Corinthians: A Commentary on the First Epistle to the Corinthians—Hermeneia* (Philadelphia: Fortress Press, 1975), 251–254.

3. David Bercot, ed., *A Dictionary of Early Christian Beliefs* (Peabody, Mass.: Hendrickson, 1998), 93–100.

Chapter 5

1. Michael Baigent, Richard Leigh, and Henry Lincoln, *Holy Blood, Holy Grail* (New York: Dell, 2004), 400.

2. Arthur F. J. Remy, *The Catholic Encyclopedia*, vol. VI, K. Knight. http://www.newadvent.org/cathen/06719a.htm.

3. Dan Brown, *Angels and Demons* (New York: Simon and Schuster, 2000), 110.

Chapter 6

1. Kurt Aland, *The Problem of the New Testament Canon* (London: Mowbray, 1962), 24.

2. Ibid., 18.

3. Phil Brennan, "Gibson: Passion Sprung from Suicide Thoughts," NewsMax.com (17 February 2004).

4. See Elaine Pagels, *The Gnostic Gospels* (New York: Random House, 1971).

5. See James Robinson, *The Nag Hammadi Library in English* (New York: Harper and Row, 1977).

6. Bertil Gärtner, *The Theology of the Gospel According to Thomas* (New York: Harper & Brothers, 1961), 11.

7. See John A. T. Robinson, *Redating the New Testament* (Philadelphia: Westminster John Knox, 1976).

8. See Colossians 2:16–19; 1 Timothy 4:1; Acts 20:29–30; 2 Peter 2:1; 1 John 2:18–19.

9. See Elaine Pagels, *Beyond Belief: The Secret Gospel of Thomas* (New York: Random House, 2003).

Chapter 7

1. See historian of western secret societies David Livingston, *The Dying God: The Hidden History of Western Civilization* (New York: Writers Club Press, 2002), 2.

2. John Van Auken, *Ancient Egyptian Mysticism and Its Relevance Today* (Virginia Beach, Va.: A.R.E. Press, 1999), 5.

3. "Circles," paragraphs 5–6. See Eugene Narrett, "Proud Ephemerals: Signs of Self-Made Men," *Culture Wars*

(December 1999), 5.

4. Ross Clifford and Philip Johnson, *Jesus and the Gods of the New Age* (Colorado Springs:Victor Books, 2003), 54.

5. Grace Gedeon, "Sacred Circle as a Psychospiritual Practice and Its Role in Creating Conscious Community," GlobalRenaissanceAlliance.com.

6. Ibid.

7. The words of Dennis Kucinich, Democratic candidate in 2004, cited in *World* (25 October 2003), 14.

8. Altreligion.about.com.

9. Ravenonline.com.

10. Fabricia's Boschetto.com.

11. Skepdic.com.

12. To our knowledge, the only time the circle has been used in orthodox Christianity is to describe the unity of God, outside of the created circle.

13. Controverscial.com.

14. LuckyMojo.com.

15. ChurchofSatan.com.

16. Helen A. Berger, Evan A. Leach, and Leigh S. Shaffer, *Voices from the Pagan Census: A National Survey of Witches and Neo-Pagans in the United States* (Columbia, S.C.: University of South Carolina Press, 2003), 21–23.

17. Elaine Pagels, *The Origin of Satan* (New York: Random House, 1995).

18. Richard Grigg, *When God Becomes Goddess: The Transformation of American Religion* (New York: Continuum, 1995), 22.

19. Jean Houston, *The Passion of Isis and Osiris: A Gateway to Transcendent Love* (New York: Ballantine, 1995), 2.

20. Hippolytus (AD170–263), in his Refutation of All Heresies 5:9:10.

21. Elinor Gadon, *The Once and Future Goddess: A Symbol for Our Time* (New York: Harper and Row, 1989).

22. Joseph Campbell, *The Power of Myth* (New York: Anchor, 1991) 58.

23. C. S. Lewis, *Miracles* (New York: MacMillan, 1947), 85, says: "The pantheist is led to state that either everything is God or that nothing is God, but in neither case is he able to give any precise meaning to his concept."

24. Wendy Hunter Roberts, *Celebrating Her: Feminist Ritualizing Comes of Age* (Cleveland, Ohio: The Pilgrim Press, 1998), see the Summer/Spring Catalog, 1999, The Pilgrim Press, the United Church of Christ publishing arm.

25. Sue Monk Kidd, *The Dance of the Dissident Daughter: A Woman's Journey from Christian Tradition to the Sacred Feminine* (San Francisco: Harper, 1996).

26. Amy Peck, "Our Mission," Center of the Sacred Feminine, http://www.sacred-feminine.org/page2.htm.

27. Mary Daly, *Beyond God the Father: Towards a Philosophy of Women's Liberation* (Boston: Beacon Press, 1973), 96.

Chapter 8

1. Bob Dylan, "Gotta Serve Somebody," © 1979 by Special Rider Music.

2. Riane Eisler, *The Chalice and the Blade: Our History, Our Future* (San Francisco: Harper and Row, 1987), 190, 194, 200. Eisler may be one of Brown's sources for this imagery.

3. Robin Lane Fox, *Pagans and Christians* (San Francisco: Harper & Row, 1986), 34. I have slightly modified the translation for the sake of clarity. This syncretism was already the case in Athens in the first century (see Acts 17).

4. Robert Turcan, *The Cults of the Roman Empire*, Antonia Nevill, trans. (Oxford, UK: Blackwell, 1996), 280.

5. Caitlín Matthews, *Sophia, Goddess of Wisdom: The Divine Feminine from Black Goddess to World Soul* (London: The Aquarian Press/Harper Collins, 1992), 330.

6. Diana L. Eck, *A New Religious America: How a "Christian Country" Has Become the World's Most Religiously Diverse Nation* (San Francisco: Harper, 2001), 77. Others have a similar goal. The

Indian Hindu philosopher, Radhakrishnan believes the "supreme task of our [present] generation … is to give a soul to our growing world consciousness," cited in ibid., 380.

7. The author of this book, Stephen Prothero, is a professor at Boston University.

8. Moshe Idel and Bernard McGinn, eds., *Mystical Union in Judaism, Christianity and Islam: An Ecumenical Dialogue* (New York: Continuum, 1996), 10–12.

9. Lewis, *Miracles*, 87. By this, Lewis means that God is not "universal being," that is, everything, because God has his own specific, determinate character.

10. Ibid., 90–91.

11. Cited in Adolf von Harnack, *Marcion: The Gospel of the Alien God*, John E. Steely and Lyle D. Bierma, trans. (Durham, N.C.: The Labyrinth Press, 1990), 72.

12. Ibid., 95.

13. Ibid., 96.

14. See Peter Jones, *Capturing the Pagan Mind*, chapters 1–4.